Washington DC

A Traveler's Guide to the
District of Columbia
and Nearby Attractions

Produced by the
Division of Publications
National Park Service

U.S. Department of the Interior
Washington, D.C. 1989

Using This Handbook

Besides being the seat of the U.S. Government, Washington, D.C., is the home of many of the Nation's major monuments and memorials. The National Park Service is entrusted with the care and interpretation of most of these cultural treasures and symbols and, beyond that, with the cultivation and tending of most of the city's parks and flower gardens. This handbook is published in support of the Park Service's management policies and interpretive programs in the National Capital Region, which includes Washington and sites in nearby Virginia, Maryland, and West Virginia. Part 1 of the handbook introduces Washington through the eyes of an adopted son from England, writer Henry Fairlie. Part 2 consists of gazetteer descriptions and illustrations of the major sites in the city and environs. Part 3 provides a thematic sampler of some obvious and not so obvious aspects of Washington and the nearby area.

National Park Handbooks, compact introductions to the great natural and historic places administered by the National Park Service, are designed to promote understanding and enjoyment of the parks. Each is intended to be informative reading and a useful guide before, during, and after a park visit. More than 100 titles are in print. They are sold at parks and can be purchased by mail from the Superintendent of Documents, U.S. Government Printing Office, Washington, DC 20402. This is Handbook 102.

Part 1

A City of Symbolic Gems

Welcome to Your Washington

By Henry Fairlie

As seen from above, the grids of Pierre L'Enfant's Plan for Washington, D.C., are evident in Freedom Plaza. Prominent to the east, down Pennsylvania Avenue, are the Old Post Office Tower and the U.S. Capitol.
Cover and pages 2-3: *Despite the near-constant activity inside, the White House enclave presents a scene of serenity and beauty at any season.*
Pages 4-5: *The afternoon sun highlights details of the Capitol dome.*

Washington is your city, wherever in the country you come from. If you come from abroad, you may also feel it is your city, for as the capital of the free world, the White House is now better known around the globe than the palaces of Europe.

Washington is a city of monuments and imposing buildings. It was laid out to be a city of grandeur. But it has miraculously kept a human scale. In this it represents the politics of a Nation in which the ordinary people are the source of power and have the final say. Even the formal stretch of the Mall, which might be as stiff as an avenue at Versailles, is used by the people of Washington as a playground. On summer evenings after work there may be several games of softball being played from the Capitol to the Washington Monument. And in early summer thousands come to the Mall for the annual Folklife Festival celebrating America's cultural diversity.

It is partly the green of the city that keeps the human scale—the Mall itself; the beautifully kept Capitol grounds; the National Arboretum, with one long high bank in spring that is a joy of brilliant azaleas among white lacy dogwoods; Dumbarton Oaks Gardens, formal, terraced, and landscaped, but falling to the wildness of Rock Creek Park; and next to them, Montrose Park, another playground of the people of the city.

Then there is the long reach of green along the Potomac, where the Mall and its monuments and museums give way to yet another playground, where the fishermen fish, the joggers pound, the picnickers picnic, the bikers ride, the walkers stroll, the sailors sail, and in summer you may even watch the mysterious game of cricket played by Englishmen who live here. The George Washington Memorial Parkway makes all this readily available on the west side of the Potomac, too.

Above all, Washington is a city in the woods. Again and again, you will find the skyline covered with

The Supreme Court building exemplifies the capital city's rich classical architecture.

trees. You can stand on the Virginia side of the 14th Street bridge and look up to the tower of Washington Cathedral, several miles away, rising on its high hill with trees clustered round it.

Running through the city is Rock Creek Park, of which Lord Bryce, a British ambassador some 80 years ago, asked in wonderment: "In what other city in the world can you walk in ten minutes into the middle of a glen?" The busy thoroughfare that now runs its length has hardly changed that aspect.

All of this and more is the backdrop to the capital city, and you should keep reminding yourself to notice it. Not only does the green soften the hard edges of what might otherwise be too monumental a city, it also helps to create an atmosphere that subdues temptations to the arrogance of power. Neither the old palaces of Europe nor the Kremlin today display any of the informality that is created by this green.

The people who exercise power and serve it are affected by this ease in their surroundings. Some of the residential districts, so close to the center of the city, are like garden suburbs: Cleveland Park, the area around Foxhall Road, and Spring Valley, which in spring lives up to its name. Across some of the streets of Georgetown the high old trees meet overhead like the nave of a cathedral. I know no great city in the world that is lovelier in the spring.

If you can spare the time, I suggest you visit Theodore Roosevelt Island, in the Potomac on the edge of the city. There used to be a ferry to it, but now you cross to it by a footbridge from the Virginia side. Since Teddy Roosevelt was the first President to really care about the environment and conservation, it was decided to keep the island in its natural state as a memorial to him. If a tree falls, it is left to rot as it would in nature; where the ground is swampy, low down by the river, it is left swampy. You can walk around the island not knowing you are near the heart of a great city.

When you spread out a map of Washington for the first time, take a moment to grasp the original design, not least the great avenues that drive diagonally across the regular grid, all with the names of states. L'Enfant's design was not fully carried through, but his stamp on the city still remains. The avenues are infuriating to cab drivers, because they keep interrupting the regular streets, so that a few blocks of a street can

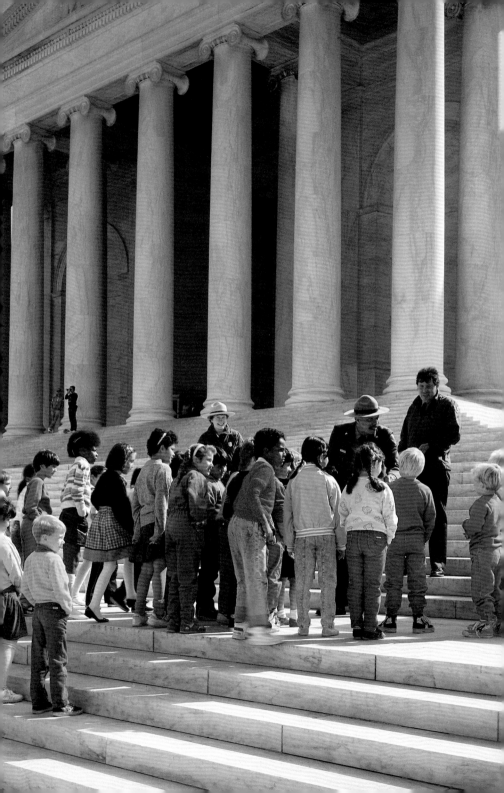

National Park Service rangers greet a group of schoolchildren visiting the Jefferson Memorial.
Pages 12-13: *Downriver from Georgetown and opposite the Kennedy Center, Theodore Roosevelt Island sits as a woodland oasis in the Potomac River.*

pop up somewhere, to disappear again, and reemerge miles away for another couple of blocks.

They can also be infuriating to the visitor, especially where avenues meet Washington's famous circles with their statues. There are ten exits from Dupont Circle, and horrifying stories are told of tourists who get into the wrong lane, can't get out of it, and just drive round in an increasing frenzy until they are quietly carried off.

One of the common jokes about Washington is that it was built on a swamp. The site was chosen to circumvent the strong claims of several states to be the home of the capital. But on this swampy place the real vision of L'Enfant was to lay out a city that could grow comfortably as the small early Republic expanded in territory, prosperity, and power "to any period however remote." The open feeling of the city today is a tribute to his foresight.

So Washington has indeed grown by leaps as the Nation's role in the world has expanded and the responsibilities of the Federal Government in a complicated modern society have increased. It grew most dramatically during the First World War, the New Deal, and the Second World War, and since then it has continued its growth. The most recent development is that Washington has become something of a business and financial center as well, partly because of the number of trade associations with their headquarters here, and partly because of the growth of the high-tech companies in the encircling suburbs.

You and your camera will know what you want to see. But as an Englishman who grew quickly to love the city when I first visited it many years ago, and who has made it his home, I may be able to whisper a few things in your ear as you set out to find your capital.

Bear in mind that, apart from the Mall, one main thoroughfare was meant to join the Capitol and the White House. This is Pennsylvania Avenue. It was intended to be the symbol of the separation of powers, the executive and legislative branches of government, under the Constitution, and also of their joining in mutual understanding and cooperation. But because of one of the corruptions of L'Enfant's design, there is a kink in Pennsylvania Avenue where the route turns up 15th Street NW for one block past the Treasury. You are certain to end up there, so take it as

yet another symbol, this time of the occasions when the cooperation between Congress and the President breaks down.

While you are at the Capitol, perhaps visiting your senators or congressman, also remember that it is here that the inauguration of the President takes place. The Chief Executive and Commander-in-Chief is confirmed in office, not in his Executive Mansion, but beneath the dome where sit the representatives of "You, the People."

You will probably find for yourself, like many visitors before you, that the loveliest view of the Capitol is from the Neptune Terrace of the Library of Congress, to which you will climb to enter the Library by its main doors. The grandeur of the building glimpsed between the trees of the Capitol grounds will catch your breath. For two centuries the hopes that a free people may govern themselves have centered on that dome.

The Library of Congress is not a branch of government. But it could well be, considering all the services it supplies to the three branches, as well as to countless other people. It is certainly one place, besides the White House, where you should take the official guided tour. The Library's activities and possessions are so numerous and fascinating that time is well spent hearing about them.

But there is again something specially American about the Library of Congress. When I first used it, I was accustomed to its equivalent in Britain, the British Museum Library, where you needed a testimonial proving you were a bona fide scholar. But not in the Library of Congress. It is the national library of a democracy. College students can and do use it on the same terms as the most serious scholars.

Next to the Library on 1st Street is the Supreme Court, the home of the third branch of government. In design it is like a temple of justice. This is wholly fitting to the grand theme of the Nation's Capital—the government of a free people—and to the exalted place given to the Constitution in the Nation's life. It is worth remembering that this lofty building was constructed during the Great Depression: there is something humanizing in the fact that the construction of this temple of the supreme law of the land gave work to unemployed Americans just as many public buildings were put up in your towns and cities.

The Great Hall in the Library of Congress is one of the most magnificent rooms in the city, if not the Nation.

14

*Pierce Mill, in Rock Creek
Park, recalls an earlier time
when hundreds of mills produced flour in Washington
and the surrounding area.*

Among the museums of the Mall there is something
for everybody, again free to the people of a democracy.
You will be struck by how many of them are run by
the Smithsonian Institution, and even they are only
part of the amazing range of its activities. There is
nothing like the Smithsonian anywhere else in the
world. It is all the more remarkable therefore that
the original endowment was bequeathed by a James
Smithson of London, the illegitimate son of a duke
of Northumberland who never even visited America
before he died in 1829.

That Smithson looked to America with such opti-
mism tells us something of the high hopes the world
had of the young Republic, and since he, as an
illegitimate child, could not succeed to his father's
title, we can only believe that he saw in America a
more tolerant country, free of the confinements of
class.

America was a breath of fresh air to the Old World
then. A hundred years later another fresh breeze was
carried by the *Spirit of St. Louis*. Stand in front of it
in the National Air and Space Museum. It looks as if
it is held together by string; it has a wicker chair in
the cockpit. Yet Lindbergh made not only America
but the whole of Europe gasp. After the fearful
devastation of the First World War, and the disillu-
sionment that followed it, this young and confident
man seemed to be the promise of the New World
arriving miraculously on the wind.

When you come to the Washington Monument
with its circle of 50 Stars and Stripes, one for each
state, which sometimes crack like rifle shots when
they whip in a stiff breeze, try to imagine the rising
ground and Ellipse below it on the Fourth of July,
when families of all races, native-born and immigrants
alike, picnic in the evening as they wait for the fireworks to begin.

Beyond is the White House. To an Englishman
used to Buckingham Palace, and the even grander
palaces of Europe, it hardly seems the home of a
head of state at all, but more like the unboastful
mansion of a country gentleman. In this, like the
modest inauguration ceremony, or the unwigged,
black-robed justices of the Supreme Court, it fits the
character of the Nation's democracy. It remains very
much the house of "We, the People" whoever
temporarily occupies it.

In Lafayette Park, Andrew Jackson salutes his troops. This monument was the first equestrian statue cast in the United States.
Pages 20-21: Sun and shadows accentuate the angular, modern lines of the National Gallery of Art East Building.

Across the street in the center of Lafayette Park is one of Washington's many statues. You might assume it is Lafayette, but no, he has a statue on one of the corners. Then surely it must be one of the Presidents on whom every President looks out. But which can it be? Look again. The horse is rearing and the figure is doffing his tricorn hat to the imaginary crowd as he easily keeps his seat. Take a guess. Why, it is Andy Jackson, truly the first people's President.

These are only a few examples of how rich Washington is in symbolism. Even the imposing buildings of Washington speak of the character of the most successful popular government the world has known. They say in a hundred ways that this is your city, as it is your Constitution, your Congress, your courts, and your President.

Then there is the rest. If Washington is not a center of contemporary culture like New York and Los Angeles, it is, as a capital should be, a treasure house of the traditional culture, including the whole past culture of Western civilization. The spirited new East Building of the National Gallery of Art should not prevent you from going to the grander original building, which houses, among other priceless works, one of the world's great collections of the old Italian masters and a roomful of Rembrandts that could itself hold you for hours. Then there are the gems the visitor finds all over Washington: the Folger Library, for example, one of the world's centers of Shakespearean studies, where Shakespeare is still performed on a reproduced Elizabethan stage; the Phillips Collection, the loveliest, warmest, most intimate small gallery I know in the world; the wonderful collection of pre-Columbian art at Dumbarton Oaks, housed in one of the most exquisite new buildings in the city; the lively summer concerts by the armed forces bands; the campuses of several universities and colleges tucked into various parts of the city; the many magnificent churches, including the massive Washington Cathedral which has been almost as long in the building as the great cathedrals of Europe; the nearly hidden beginning of the 185-mile C&O Canal in Georgetown.

Beyond the District's boundaries but easily accessible is still more. Nothing is more moving, or perhaps closer to the heart of the Nation, than Arlington National Cemetery, with the graves of John F. Kennedy

19

Students enjoy a sunny day at Georgetown University. Academic life flourishes here, for the Washington area's many universities and colleges attract students from across the United States and abroad.

and his brother Robert F. Kennedy and with Arlington House, the old Custis-Lee mansion, overlooking the city. But it is the ranks and ranks of plain headstones, the graves of the unfamous, the unsung dead of the wars fought to keep America free, that are the reason you should go there. And if you stand at the top of the steep hill and look down over the headstones, your eyes will fall first and with some irony on the fortress of the Pentagon.

There is Mount Vernon, so easy to reach, and again it is the modesty of the home that is striking. This man who twice saved his country, as soldier and then as statesman, who set it securely on its path to freedom and not monarchy or dictatorship, lived in this home he loved, but left so often, the simple life of a country gentleman. Georgetown with its red-bricked streets may be within the District, but historic Alexandria lies just over the river in Virginia. In the surrounding countryside of Virginia are the reminders of the colony that contributed four of the first five Presidents of the United States. Within an easy drive is one of the smaller but still gracious colonial mansions, the home of George Mason, the father of the Bill of Rights.

In Virginia, Maryland, and nearby West Virginia are many Civil War sites—Antietam, Manassas, Fredericksburg, Harpers Ferry—and you may easily in a day thrust into Pennsylvania to the battlefield of Gettysburg where as you look on the rugged ground you can well imagine the terrible savagery of the fighting.

Also well within reach is Annapolis with its old Colonial streets and wharfs and the splendid campus of the Naval Academy, and there you are also at the great opening expanse of the Chesapeake Bay, with the thrill—but not in the traffic at the end of a holiday—of crossing its great bridge. There are even Washingtonians who go for the day by car or train to Baltimore, a city and port rich in character and history. Some drive there at night, as even a tourist may wish to do, to see the Orioles, who are loved by their fans whether they win or lose at baseball.

All the time on your visit to the Nation's Capital you will be largely in the care of the National Park Service. I have wondered at the dedication and skill of the Park Service when I've been on the top of the Rockies in the cold wind on a midsummer's day. The discreet notices of the Park Service along the trail to the top of one mountain give you all the information you want about the ecology and the necessary warning that it is so fragile in such a harsh environment that even if you just stray from the trail, perhaps first beaten by Indians, you might damage it.

The activity of that same National Park Service in Washington and surrounding Virginia and Maryland is equally remarkable. It manages the major tourist sites, including the Mall and the Ellipse. It looks after much of the green of Washington, the many flower beds and plots of grass that are like a hundred lungs for the city. It takes care of the building, furnishings, and grounds of the White House; maintains the John F. Kennedy and Wolf Trap Farm Park performing arts centers; it keeps the Theodore Roosevelt Island I have mentioned—and appropriately so, for the National Park Service was established in 1916 largely due to his earlier initiatives.

So one could go on; the Vietnam Veterans Memorial is only one of the most recent National Park System sites that fill this guide. But I may be allowed to say that I know no similar service in any country in the world that undertakes the responsibility for so many and such a wide variety of places, from coast to coast, with such attention to both maintaining the integrity of the sites and making welcome the more than 200 million people of the American democracy.

If you go to Theodore Roosevelt Island, there is a stone memorial to T.R., and as befits the man it is monumental. The great slabs of stone carry quotations from some of his speeches. Read them, even photograph them, they are inspiring. When you go to the absolutely perfect memorial to Abraham Lincoln, read the quotations from his speeches as well. Even read them aloud, especially the passage from his Second Inaugural about binding the wounds of the Nation. At the end of one Thanksgiving evening with some Americans, we all clambered into a car, drove by the floodlit monuments of Washington at night— you should do that as well—and at the Lincoln Memorial, one of the Americans said to me, "You read that aloud." I did, and at the end we all were silent. Silent but unembarrassed to belong to a Nation to which a self-taught boy could speak the soul of America across the years. I relate that incident only to ask you to keep your eyes up and open wherever

Pershing Park, located in front of the restored Willard Hotel near the main business district, is one of the city's many havens of greenery maintained by the National Park Service.

Pages 26-27: Amidst the hustle and bustle of Pennsylvania Avenue, three travelers from abroad relax for a few moments in Pershing Park's quietude.

Pages 28-29: The Jefferson Memorial reflects the architectural tastes of the man it honors. Drafter of the Declaration of Independence and third U.S. President, Thomas Jefferson played a leading role in the creation of the federal city.

The Reflecting Pool embellishes an autumn sunset at Lincoln Memorial.
Pages 32-33: At the National Archives, the Nation's important documents are on display for all to see.

you go in this city. There are so many small things to notice. Read the inscriptions above the two entrances to the National Archives and read the inscriptions at the main entrance to the Smithsonian's National Museum of American History.

Look at the busts above the main entrance to the Library of Congress, and then the names of the writers, philosophers, and scientists round the magnificent ceiling of its main lobby. Look even at the lamps outside the Library; you'll rarely see street lamps so beautiful or fanciful. Look at the spouting fountain that gives the Neptune Terrace its name, and look at the many other fountains in the city. Look at the statues, many of them on the circles, but not all; you will find Longfellow brooding among the swirling traffic at M and Connecticut.

And in the end you will come back to three pieces of paper. When I was first taken to the National Archives by an American, it was with awe that I joked that the Declaration of Independence, the Constitution, and the Bill of Rights seemed to be set out as if they were on an altar. So they are. So they should be. No other nation in the beginning put so much trust in three pieces of paper. No other three pieces of paper have through 200 testing years so proved they deserved that trust. That these documents are not dead but alive is what everything you see in Washington is telling you—and, through you, the rest of the world. Why do the immigrants, of whom Washington has its share, still come? For the same reasons your ancestors, many of whom were immigrants, once came.

Come down Massachusetts Avenue from Washington Cathedral, past all the embassies of the world, and remember how small a country of merchants and farmers started this experiment in democracy more than two centuries ago. It is a capital of which any American can be proud. As I have noticed every spring and summer, the tourists are indeed proud, proud even of the efficiency, cleanness, and dignity of the Metro subway. That Washingtonians keep the stations and the cars so clean says something of their own pride in their city. In a way, we keep this city for you, and we like it when you come. In summer I like to walk along the Mall and look at the license plates of the cars and campers. They seem to come from every state of the Union. And I like to look at the

families who arrive in these cars and campers making what might be their once-in-a-lifetime pilgrimage to the Nation's Capital. Their diversity is truly remarkable, and yet they all are sharing a common trek, a visit to the memorials, monuments, and other traditional landmarks that unite them as one people. Tourism may be business in most places, but in Washington, it is more than that. Here, tourism is also the spirited enjoyment with which you come to see the city, and your enjoyment invigorates us as we go about our day-to-day chores.

Let me leave you with one last thought. The American artist Georgia O'Keeffe said that perhaps we will never again build cities as lovely as Venice or Florence. But they are now, she said, only conversation pieces. The life is in the cities of America. The wonder of Washington is that, artificially created as a capital, there is nothing artificial about it. It has grown with the Nation in response to the same impulses. I believe you will at once feel at home in it. For it is yours.

Washington is a city of celebrations, and most splendiferous of all is the Fourth of July fireworks show on the Washington Monument grounds.

Part 2

Gazetteer for Travelers

We're Here to Help You

Washington, in all its splendor and variety, welcomes you whether you are here for a day, a week, or longer. The city's attractions are so numerous that you will be challenged by the choices you have to make. Nearly every visitor first wants to see the Nation's primary symbols—the Capitol, the White House, and the Supreme Court—and to tour the National Mall with its well-known museums and landmarks.

At these places you will find a familiar face and friendly hand, for most of the monuments, memorials, and parks in the Nation's Capital are maintained and managed by the very same National Park Service that has come to be identified with the country's natural, historical, and recreational wonders: Yellowstone, Grand Canyon, and nearly 340 other sites. In fact, many of Washington's parks are among the Nation's oldest, for they date from the District of Columbia's establishment in 1790.

Besides the memorials and monuments, the National Park Service manages many small and lesser-known sites here ranging from Old Stone House in Georgetown to Kenilworth Aquatic Gardens on the banks of the Anacostia River. Wherever you travel, you will meet and be met by the men and women of the National Park Service in their familiar uniforms. They are taking care of these parks and monuments and helping travelers like yourself in the tradition of the National Park Service, so do not hesitate to ask these park rangers, maintenance workers, and mounted park policemen for assistance. They will do all they can to answer your questions and to help you make the most of your visit. The following gazetteer, packed with details about the Washington area's major sites, is offered with that same friendly spirit. Use it as your guide.

Tips for Travelers

More than 18 million tourists come to Washington each year. That's a lot of people, but the facilities for providing travel information to these people and for answering their questions are numerous and widespread.

Each major airport, such as Washington-Dulles International (above) where many visitors arrive, has trained staff members on hand to deal with travelers' problems.

The National Park Service staffs two kiosks—on the Ellipse and near the Vietnam Veterans Memorial—that are open all year to provide information and to help visitors. Other kiosks are open seasonally.

The International Visitors Information Service (IVIS), Suite 300, 733 15th Street, NW, provides brochures and information on accommodations and the highlights of the city; 783-6540.

The Washington Convention and Visitors Association, 1575 I Street, NW, operates an information center at 1455 Pennsylvania Avenue, NW; 789-7000.

Climate
Washington has four distinct seasons. Spring is beautiful and alive with the fresh greens and bright colors of blooming flowers and shrubs. Summer is hot, humid, and often hazy. Fall may bring the nicest weather with bright sunny days and cool northwest breezes. Winter is usually cold and damp with several storms and at least one major snowfall that can turn this northernmost of southern cities into quite a mess.

Crossing State Lines
The Washington Metropolitan Area spreads into two states, Maryland and Virginia, besides taking up all of the District of Columbia. This means that the

sales tax rate differs, that street and directional signs vary, and that local regulations are different.

Access for the Disabled
Many sites and programs in metropolitan Washington, D.C., are accessible to the disabled. Tourmobile Sightseeing Services offers an accessible van available on 24-hour notice; call 554-7020. For information on accessibility and for a list of TDD numbers, call 426-5264 (TDD) or 426-6770 (voice). For information about the Smithsonian, check with the Office of Education, 357-1697 (voice), 357-1696 (TDD).

Airports
The Washington area is served by three major airports. Washington National, for domestic flights, is located on the banks of the Potomac, near Alexan-

Theater Tickets

Tickets are available at each theater box office and through Ticketron, which accepts orders over the telephone. Ticketplace provides day-of-performance tickets, when available, at half price from a booth on the F Street Plaza between 12th and 13th Streets, NW. Payment must be in cash. (See The Performing Arts, pages 148-49.)

Spectator Sports

For years tickets for the Washington Redskins home games have been sold out, so television is your only resort if you do not have a friend with tickets. Tickets for the Bullets, the professional basketball team, and the Capitals, the professional hockey team, are not as hard to come by, but they are in great demand. The closest major league baseball team is the Orioles in Baltimore.

dria, Virginia, a short Metro-rail ride from downtown. Washington-Dulles International, 27 miles west in Virginia, and Baltimore-Washington International, 20 miles northeast toward Baltimore, have both domestic and international flights. Shuttle buses operate to all three airports from major hotels and motels downtown and in the suburbs.

Trains

Amtrak serves Union Station (above) on Capitol Hill with trains to and from cities all over the Nation. The Maryland Department of Transportation operates commuter trains from the station.

Interstate Buses

Greyhound/Trailways Bus Lines serves the city from a station at 1005 1st Street, NE.

Getting Around the City

Planning your excursions around Washington can be an important part of your visit, for parking is often difficult and can be very frustrating, especially on hot, summer days. The District of Columbia police do not hesitate to give tickets—the penalties are high for parking violations, and offenders may have cars towed. You might consider parking your car in the suburbs and taking public transportation downtown. When you leave your car, either take valuables with you or leave them locked in your trunk. Alternatives to using your car in the downtown area are outlined on these two pages, and you may wish to consider one or more of them before you begin your excursion.

How the City Is Laid Out

First off, you should know that Washington is divided into four parts: Northwest, Northeast, Southeast, and Southwest. North Capitol, East Capitol, and South Capitol Streets and the Mall to the west divide the city into these quadrants (see map on pages 46-47). East-west streets carry the letters of the alphabet in alphabetical order as they move away from the center. There are no B, J, X, Y, or Z Streets. After W Street come two-syllable names, again in alphabetical order. They are followed by three syllable names, and finally at the furthest extreme of the city are streets named for plants and trees. North-south streets are simply numbered, again beginning at the center. Since there is, for example, a 4th Street in each quadrant, make sure you check whether the address is followed by NW, NE, SE, or SW. But that's not the end of it. What jumbles this system are the avenues, drives, and streets—named after all the states except Washington—that crisscross the city, disrupting the grid and creating oddly shaped intersections.

Subways and Buses

The Washington Metropolitan Area Transit Authority, known locally as Metro, operates the subways and buses. Metrorail—the subway—serves more than 60 stations at present and, besides crisscrossing the downtown, extends into the Maryland and Virginia suburbs. All stations—identified by a pylon topped with an "M"—and trains are accessible for handicapped persons in wheelchairs. Metrorail operates 5:30 a.m. to midnight Monday through Friday, 8 a.m. to midnight on Saturday, and 10 a.m. to midnight on Sunday. You need a farecard to ride the subway, and these can be purchased from machines in every

Getting Around the Mall

Tourmobile

If you are planning to spend one or more days touring the museums and monuments near the National Mall, consider using the Tourmobile (left). This is a National Park Service concessioner-operated, narrated sightseeing bus service that stops at all major points of interest on the Mall, Capitol Hill, and Arlington Cemetery. Tickets allow unlimited reboarding privileges and can be purchased from the driver as you board; only travelers checks and cash are accepted. Children under 3 ride free; children 3 through 11 ride at a reduced fare. Service to Frederick Douglass National Historic Site is available June 15 to Labor Day and to Mount Vernon April through October. Buses run 9 a.m. to 6:30 p.m. from mid-June to Labor Day and 9:30 a.m. to 4:30 p.m. the rest of the year.

station for amounts up to $20. Put the farecard into the turnstile as you enter and leave a station. Fares are determined by the length of the ride and the time of day, with rush-hour charges the highest. You can get transfers to the bus system that eliminate or reduce the fare. Transfers from one bus to another result in no additional fare. Always pick up transfers as you begin your trip. A Weekend Tourist Pass allows unlimited travel on both buses and subways for up to four people on Saturdays, Sundays, and holidays at a reduced fare. The pass can be bought at

Metro Center, the Pentagon station, Metro headquarters, and at all bus depots. Some hotels have them available for guests.

Taxis

Taxis provide an alternative to public transportation and your own car. Fares inside the District of Columbia are determined by zones and the amount is based on the number of zone boundaries crossed. If you are in doubt about the zone system, ask the driver in advance about the fare to be charged. Taxis in Maryland and Virginia operate on meters.

Looking West down the Mall

Using This Gazetteer

This gazetteer is organized to help you make the best use of your time in Washington, D.C., and its environs and to provide you with enough information about the various sites that you can make an informed choice about what to see in the time you have available. Part 2—what you are reading now—is divided into three broad groups—Downtown East, Downtown West, and the Metropolitan Area.

How the Gazetteer Is Organized

The entries describing sites in the first two categories—Downtown East and Downtown West—are assembled into loose geographical order, so you can probably reach any four or five of them easily on foot. And that is something important to remember, for Washington is a very walkable city. Nice wide sidewalks and

relatively level terrain make this possible. Downtown East begins with the U.S. Capitol, circles around Capitol Hill, takes in sites north of the Federal Triangle—that piece of land enclosed by Constitution Avenue, Pennsylvania Avenue, and 15th Street where many government offices are located—and then goes counter-clockwise around the Mall through the various Smithsonian Institution museums, ending up with the National Archives and the National Gallery of Art. Downtown West starts at the Ellipse and then the White House, takes in the sites north and west of Lafayette Park, and finishes with the memorials to George Washington, Thomas Jefferson, and Abraham Lincoln. The Metropolitan Area section consists of sites outside the Downtown area but within or near the Capital Beltway. This is sub-

divided into the three political subdivisions—the District of Columbia, Maryland, and Virginia—and the sites are listed alphabetically within each group.

To recapitulate: the sites in the downtown core are listed geographically and those outside this central core are presented in alphabetical order.

The Descriptions

The gazetteer entries contain the address and the times and days of the week that the site is open. If there is an admission fee, it is noted along with any special facilities, tour arrangements, or provisions for the handicapped. Though restaurants and cafes to suit all palates and pockets are abundant throughout the city and many government buildings have cafeterias, food service at individual sites is noted in each entry. Museum shops are also men-

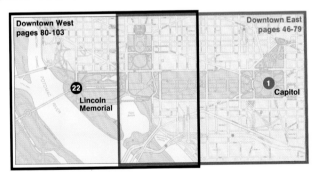

Downtown West
pages 80-103

Downtown East
pages 46-79

22 Lincoln Memorial

1 Capitol

POTOMAC RIVER

The Maps

This guidebook contains four maps to help you find the places that are mentioned in the text. Each site in Part 2 has a number that is shown in a circle at the beginning of the gazetteer entry and on the respective map. The circles for the Downtown East entries are red; the map is on pages 46-47. Those for Downtown West are black; that map is on pages 80-81. The Metropolitan Area map is on page 104; its circles are green. The fourth map is on page 158. It is intended to arouse your curiosity with an indication of the variety and diversity of side trips you could take throughout the area from Philadelphia, Pennsylvania, to Norfolk, Virginia.

tioned. A brief description of each site completes the entry. Occasionally a detailed discussion—a feature—follows an entry, giving background information on the site.

Although this gazetteer accents places managed by the National Park Service, it includes as many other sites as possible regardless of whatever public or private authority administers them, and that

selection is representative of the wealth of museums, parks, and historic homes to be found here in and around the Nation's Capital.

Once you have become familiar with the area, venture out on your own. You may discover a gem or two by yourself that we have missed—and have the pleasant surprise of stumbling onto something thoroughly enjoyable.

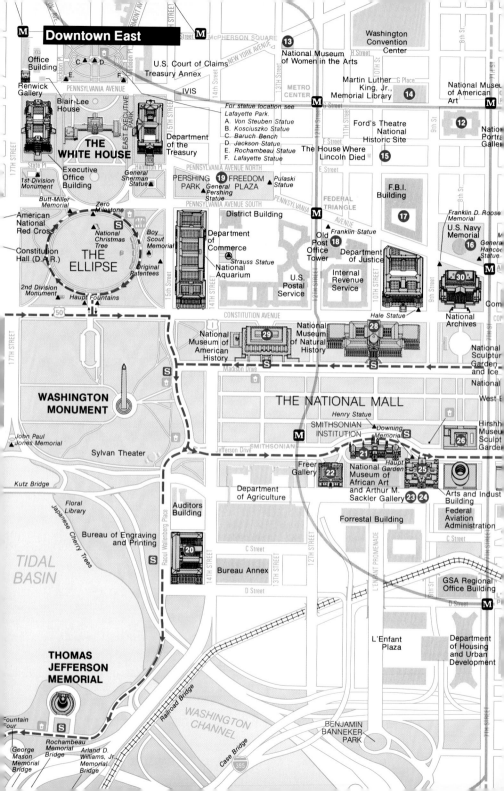

Downtown East

For statue location see
Lafayette Park.
A. Von Steuben Statue
B. Kosciuszko Statue
C. Baruch Bench
D. Jackson Statue
E. Rochambeau Statue
F. Lafayette Statue

Office Building

U.S. Court of Claims
Treasury Annex

National Museum
of Women in the Arts

Washington
Convention
Center

Renwick Gallery

IVIS

Martin Luther
King, Jr.,
Memorial Library

National Museu
of American
Art

Blair-Lee
House

THE WHITE HOUSE

Department
of the
Treasury

Ford's Theatre
National
Historic Site

Natio
Porta
Galle

Executive
Office
Building

General
Sherman
Statue

The House Where
Lincoln Died

1st Division
Monument

Butt-Miller
Memorial

Zero
Milestone

PERSHING
PARK

FREEDOM
PLAZA

Pulaski
Statue

General
Pershing
Statue

American
National
Red Cross

National
Christmas
Tree

Boy
Scout
Memorial

District Building

F.B.I.
Building

Franklin D. Roose
Memorial

Constitution
Hall (D.A.R.)

THE
ELLIPSE

Original
Patentees

Department
of
Commerce

Franklin
Statue

Old
Post
Office
Tower

Department
of
Justice

U.S. Navy
Memorial

Gene
Hancoc
Statue

2nd Division
Monument

Haupt Fountains

National
Aquarium

Strauss Statue

U.S.
Postal
Service

Internal
Revenue
Service

FEDERAL
TRIANGLE

National
Archives

National
Sculptur
Garden
and Ice

CONSTITUTION AVENUE

Hale Statue

National
Museum of
American
History

National
Museum
of Natural
History

WASHINGTON
MONUMENT

Madison Drive

THE NATIONAL MALL

National
West E

John Paul
Jones Memorial

Sylvan Theater

Henry Statue

SMITHSONIAN
INSTITUTION

Downing
Memorial

Hirshh
Museu
Sculpt
Garde

Kutz Bridge

Jefferson Drive

SMITHSONIAN

Freer
Gallery

Floral
Library

National
Garden

Haupt
Garden

Auditors
Building

Department
of
Agriculture

National
Museum of
African Art
and Arthur M.
Sackler Gallery

Arts and Indust
Building

Bureau of Engraving
and Printing

Federal
Aviation
Administration

TIDAL
BASIN

C Street

Forrestal Building

Bureau Annex

D Street

L'Enfant
Plaza

GSA Regional
Office Building

THOMAS
JEFFERSON
MEMORIAL

Department
of Housing
and Urban
Development

Fountain
our

George
Mason
Memorial
Bridge

Rochambeau
Memorial Bridge

Arland D.
Williams, Jr.
Memorial
Bridge

Railroad Bridge

WASHINGTON
CHANNEL

BENJAMIN
BANNEKER
PARK

Case Bridge

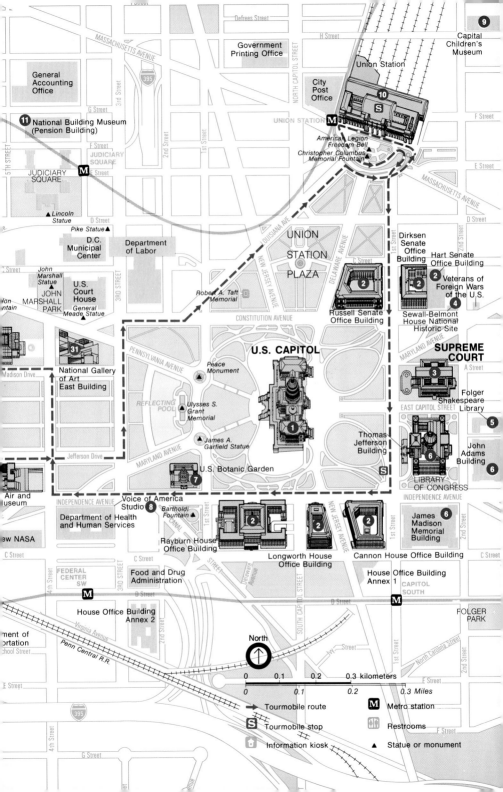

Fulton Street

Defrees Street

H Street

⑨ Capital Children's Museum

Government Printing Office

Union Station

General Accounting Office

City Post Office

MASSACHUSETTS AVENUE

⑩ S

UNION STATION

F Street

⑪ National Building Museum (Pension Building)

G Street

3rd Street

2nd Street

1st Street

NORTH CAPITOL STREET

M

American Legion Freedom Bell

Christopher Columbus Memorial Fountain

E Street

F Street

E Street

JUDICIARY SQUARE

M

2nd Street

MASSACHUSETTS AVENUE

D Street

JUDICIARY SQUARE

▲ Lincoln Statue

Pike Statue ▲

D.C. Municipal Center

Department of Labor

D Street

LOUISIANA AVE.

UNION STATION PLAZA

DELAWARE AVENUE

1st Street

C Street

Dirksen Senate Office Building

Hart Senate Office Building

2nd Street

D Street

John Marshall Statue

JOHN MARSHALL PARK

U.S. Court House

General Meade Statue ▲

3RD STREET

Robert A. Taft Memorial

NEW JERSEY AVENUE

CONSTITUTION AVENUE

② Russell Senate Office Building

② Veterans of Foreign Wars of the U.S. ④

Sewall-Belmont House National Historic Site

MARYLAND AVENUE

SUPREME COURT

③

Folger Shakespeare Library ⑤

National Gallery of Art East Building

③①

PENNSYLVANIA AVENUE

Peace Monument ▲

U.S. CAPITOL

A Street

Madison Drive

REFLECTING POOL

Ulysses S. Grant Memorial ▲

EAST CAPITOL STREET

⑥

John Adams Building ⑥

Air and Museum

Jefferson Drive

▲ James A. Garfield Statue

MARYLAND AVENUE

Thomas Jefferson Building

⑥

LIBRARY OF CONGRESS

U.S. Botanic Garden ⑦

S

INDEPENDENCE AVENUE

Voice of America Studio ⑧

Bartholdi Fountain ▲

INDEPENDENCE AVENUE

Department of Health and Human Services

New NASA

② Rayburn House Office Building

② Longworth House Office Building

② Cannon House Office Building

James Madison Memorial Building ⑥

1st Street

C Street

C Street

FEDERAL CENTER SW

M

Food and Drug Administration

House Office Building Annex 1

CAPITOL SOUTH

FOLGER PARK

4th STREET

3RD STREET

2nd Street

D Street

SOUTH CAPITOL STREET

D Street

1st Street

M

2nd Street

House Office Building Annex 2

Virginia Avenue

ment of ortation

chool Street

Penn Central R.R.

E Street

North

0   0.1   0.2   0.3 kilometers
0   0.1   0.2   0.3 Miles

→ Tourmobile route

M Metro station

S Tourmobile stop

🚻 Restrooms

ℹ Information kiosk

▲ Statue or monument

4th STREET

G Street

❶ U.S. Capitol, Capitol Hill. The Capitol is open daily 9 a.m. to 4:30 p.m. Closed January 1, Thanksgiving, and December 25. For security reasons all persons and anything that they may be carrying are examined as they enter the building. Guided tours of the historic parts of the Capitol begin in the Rotunda every few minutes from 9 a.m. to 3:45 p.m. Information on committee meetings and hearings is available daily. If you wish to go to the visitors' gallery in either chamber without taking the tour, you may obtain passes from your Senators or Representative. And you may walk around the Capitol's public areas without joining a tour. Restaurants and snack bars are located in the Capitol and in each of the office buildings. The Public Dining Room on the Senate side of

the Capitol and the Longworth Cafeteria are always open to the public; all others are restricted to staff members during the lunch hour when Congress is in session. Facilities for the handicapped are available throughout the building, including special tours for the hearing impaired and for the blind or visually impaired.

History is made every day in the Capitol, the nerve center of American Government. At no other location in Washington is the democratic process so visible. Here the people's elected representatives make daily decisions that affect the lives of every person living in this Nation. Within this wealth of activity, some actions stand out from all the rest. For instance, it was here in the Old Senate Chamber that Daniel Webster, Henry Clay, and John C.

Calhoun debated the merits of the Federal Union during their long public careers. After 1859, this was the home of the Supreme Court for 76 years. In Statuary Hall, which was the Old House Chamber, a small disk on the floor marks the spot where John Quincy Adams was fatally stricken while denouncing the Nation's involvement in the Mexican War in 1848. In the House of Representatives, Presidents have delivered their State of the Union addresses. Here, too, Woodrow Wilson in 1917 and Franklin Roosevelt in 1941 asked Congress for Declarations of War. Most Presidents, too, have been inaugurated at the Capitol. On December 9, 1824, the members rose to greet the marquis de Lafayette as he came to visit the Capitol of the Nation he had helped create. Over the years

Statue of Freedom

the remains of a few eminent individuals have lain in state in the Rotunda. The first so honored was Henry Clay, Senator from Kentucky, Secretary of State, and frequent presidential candidate. He was followed by Abraham Lincoln in 1865. In recent years Presidents John Kennedy, Herbert Hoover, Dwight Eisenhower, and Lyndon Johnson have been accorded this honor. Besides the momentous events, the ordinary business of government proceeds every day in the various committee and meeting rooms located throughout the building. These hearings often lead to new legislation or investigate the possibility of the misuse of power. A few events not strictly within the realm of government but of importance to the Nation have taken place here. One of the most momentous was when Samuel F. B. Morse tapped out the first telegraph message, "What hath God wrought?" from the Capitol to his assistant in Baltimore in 1844. The Capitol grounds are as splendid as the building. Trees from more than two-thirds of the states grow here. One tree, a mountain maple, is registered with the American Forestry Association as a champion for its species. Three trees—two English elms and one American elm—are known to have been here before work began on the Capitol. The grounds are the result of design work by Frederick Law Olmsted. Starting in 1874 Olmsted reworked the soil of the grounds plowing and replowing, adding compost, swamp muck, ground oyster shells, and lime. Now 100 species of trees and shrubs beautify the grounds.

49

The Capitol: Centerpiece of the Capital

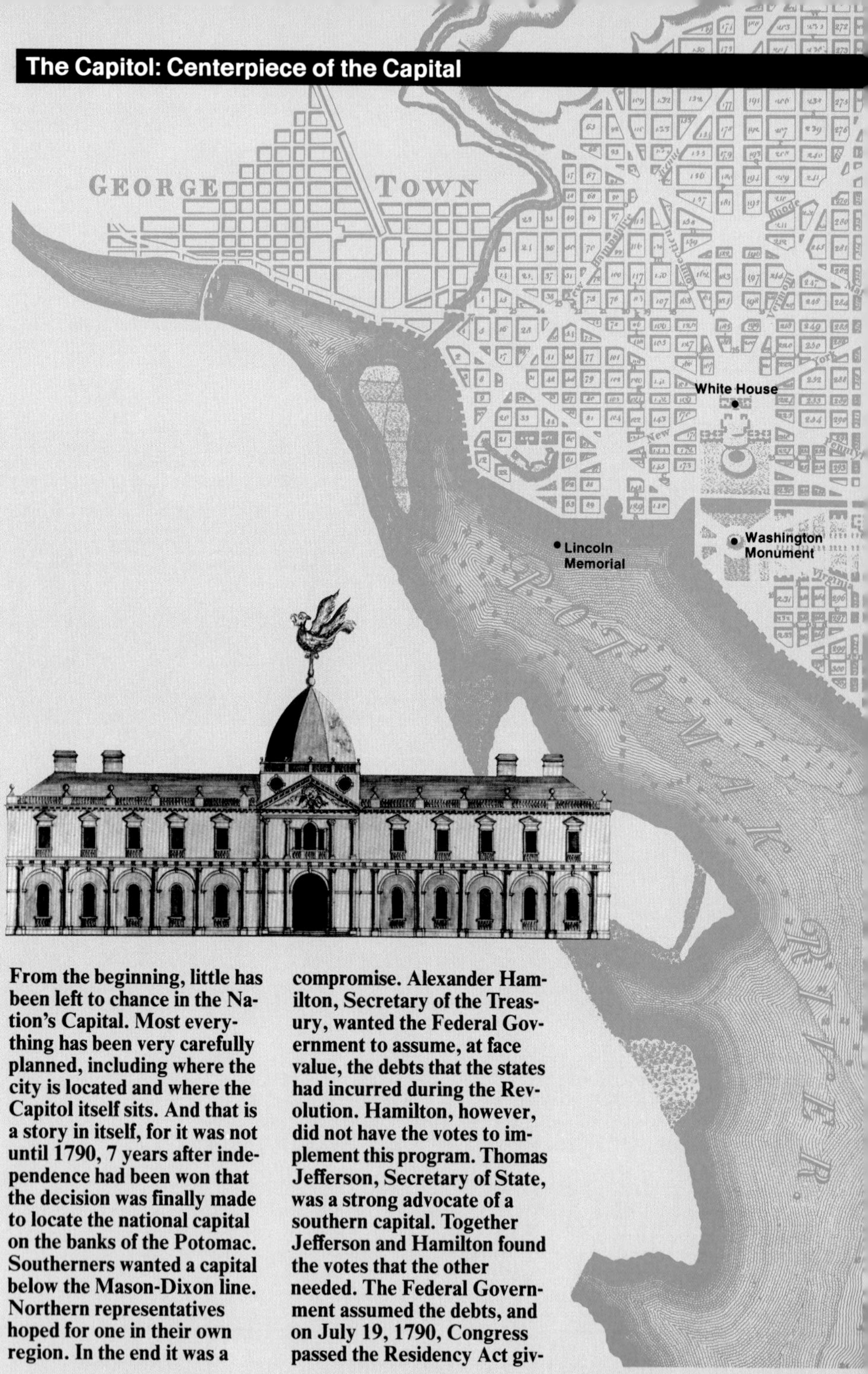
GEORGE TOWN
White House
Lincoln Memorial
Washington Monument
POTOMAK RIVER

From the beginning, little has been left to chance in the Nation's Capital. Most everything has been very carefully planned, including where the city is located and where the Capitol itself sits. And that is a story in itself, for it was not until 1790, 7 years after independence had been won that the decision was finally made to locate the national capital on the banks of the Potomac. Southerners wanted a capital below the Mason-Dixon line. Northern representatives hoped for one in their own region. In the end it was a compromise. Alexander Hamilton, Secretary of the Treasury, wanted the Federal Government to assume, at face value, the debts that the states had incurred during the Revolution. Hamilton, however, did not have the votes to implement this program. Thomas Jefferson, Secretary of State, was a strong advocate of a southern capital. Together Jefferson and Hamilton found the votes that the other needed. The Federal Government assumed the debts, and on July 19, 1790, Congress passed the Residency Act giv-

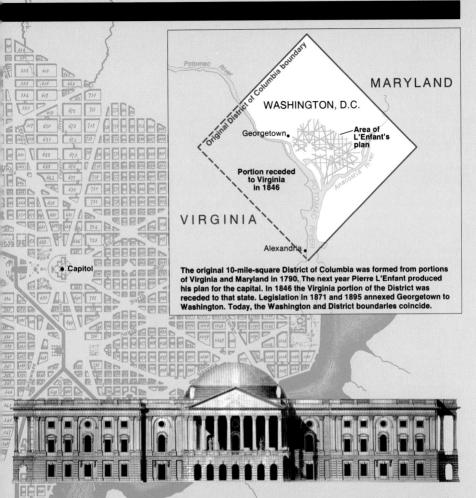

MARYLAND

Potomac River

WASHINGTON, D.C.

Original District of Columbia boundary

Georgetown.

Area of
L'Enfant's
plan

Portion receded
to Virginia
in 1846

Anacostia River

VIRGINIA

POTOMAC RIVER

Alexandria.

• Capitol

The original 10-mile-square District of Columbia was formed from portions
of Virginia and Maryland in 1790. The next year Pierre L'Enfant produced
his plan for the capital. In 1846 the Virginia portion of the District was
receded to that state. Legislation in 1871 and 1895 annexed Georgetown to
Washington. Today, the Washington and District boundaries coincide.

ing President George Washington the authority to pick the location for the federal capital on the Potomac River (see inset map). After selecting the site, Washington chose French engineer Pierre L'Enfant to lay out the city. The plan produced here is by Andrew Ellicott, L'Enfant's surveyor, who was aided by Benjamin Bannecker, a free black. Once the plan was in hand the commissioners held a competition for the design of the most important structure, the Capitol, which L'Enfant had sited on Jenkins Hill, a point with vistas to the west and south. Dr. William Thornton, a physician and amateur architect, won with a plan calling for a structure of classical proportions with a shallow dome (above, right). Among the other proposals was one (above, left) by James Diamond. On September 18, 1793, Washington laid the cornerstone. When the Senate Chamber was finished, Congress moved from Philadelphia and met in Washington for the first time on November 21, 1800.

The Evolving Capitol

Looking at the drawings Dr. William Thornton submitted for the Capitol, it is hard to see exactly where his building is today, for it has been re-shaped, altered, and enlarged by his successors as the Nation's needs and priorities have changed. When Congress moved from Philadelphia, only the Senate Chamber was finished. The Senate, House of Representatives, Supreme Court, and the courts of the District of Columbia shared these cramped quarters until the House of Representatives Chamber was completed in 1807. At that time the two chambers were connected by a covered wooden walkway. After the building was burned by the British in 1814, architect Benjamin Henry Latrobe, who had been supervising construction since 1803, threw himself into the work of re-building. In 1817 Charles Bulfinch took over and stayed on the job until the Capitol was finished in 1829, leaving the Capitol looking as it did in this 1844 painting by William MacLeod. Even as the construction came to an end, however, the demands of the fast-growing Nation were making the need for more space inevitable. In 1850 money was set aside for new and larger Senate and House wings. Thomas U. Walter was chosen as the architect, and the cornerstone for the addition was laid the next year. When the Statue of Freedom by Thomas Crawford was lifted atop the new dome on December 2, 1863, the Capitol assumed the basic form we know today. Between 1958 and 1962 the central portion of the East Front was extended to provide additional office space, but the facade's design remained unchanged. In the mid-1980s, the original, crumbling sandstone of the West Front was restored and strengthened, ensuring the structure's survival into its third century.

Nations do not only live in the present or the future. The past shows them where they have been and what they have tried to do. It is appropriate that these twin threads of a Nation's sense of being find expression in this Capitol building where so much activity concerns the future while searching for guideposts in the past. Through various forms of art—paintings, portraits, frescoes, statues, busts, reliefs, murals, friezes—the great men and women and the paramount events of our history are honored. The

most splendid space in the Capitol is the Rotunda. The cast iron dome soars above the floor culminating in Constantino Brumidi's fresco (left) of "The Apotheosis of Washington," on which the artist worked 11 months. At the base of the dome a frieze, designed and begun by Brumidi, is painted to look like a bas-relief and depicts key moments in American history. Both the frieze and the canopy under the dome were cleaned and conserved in 1987. Paintings by major artists are set into the Rotunda walls. Statues and busts of prominent Americans are located around the floor. The bronze doors at the eastern entrance to the Rotunda depict the life of Christopher Columbus. Statuary Hall is one of the best known features of the Capitol. In 1864 Congress decided that each state should send to the Capitol a bronze or marble statue of an individual noted "for their historic renown" with a limit of two statues per state. Many statues are in the Old House chamber; others are located throughout the building. All through the Capitol decoration abounds. A few artists – Brumidi in the 19th-century and Allyn Cox in the 20th – spent years painting historic events, Americans at work, the native flora and fauna, and allegorical scenes. Everywhere you look, you will find art. In the older parts of the Capitol look for the column capitals. Instead of the traditional Greek and Roman decoration you will find ears of corn and tobacco leaves and flowers designed by Benjamin Henry Latrobe.

② Senate and House Office Buildings, Capitol Hill. Open 9 a.m. to 5 p.m. Monday through Friday. Closed January 1, Thanksgiving, December 25, and weekends. The office buildings are linked to the Capitol by an underground train that the public may ride although the legislators have preference when going to vote. If you want to watch the House or Senate at work, you need a free visitor's pass. For admission to the gallery of the House of Representatives you should go to your Congressman's of-

fice. For tickets to the Senate, go to either of your Senators. Should you wish to make a business appointment with your Representative or Senators, see the receptionist, who will set up one if possible. Read the local newspapers, for they print schedules of activities in both houses and of the various committees.

South of the Capitol, on Independence Avenue, are the three office buildings of the House of Representatives. On the north side, on Constitution Avenue, are the Senate office buildings.

③ Supreme Court of the United States, East Capitol and First Streets, NE. Open 9 a.m. to 4:30 p.m. Monday through Friday. Closed weekends and holidays. Limited seating is available to the public on a first-come, first-served basis. Short courtroom presentations are held every hour on the half hour from 9:30 a.m. to 3:30 p.m. except when the Court hears oral arguments. On days the Court sits only to hand down opinions, presentations begin at 11:30 a.m. The ground floor has changing exhibits on the Court and

the Justices and a 30-minute film. Food service.

"The Republic endures and this is the symbol of its faith," said Chief Justice Charles Evans Hughes as he laid the cornerstone for the Supreme Court's first permanent home in 1932. During the previous 145 years, the Court had met in Manhattan's Royal Exchange Building, the Philadelphia City Hall, the basement of the U.S. Capitol, a tavern, the Old Senate Chamber, and a few other places. To provide the Court with its own building Chief Justice William Howard Taft labored long and hard. The white marble structure, designed by Cass Gilbert in the style of a classic Greek temple, displays the legend "Equal Justice Under Law." On both sides of the main stairway leading to the building are massive statues. One represents "The Contemplation of Justice" and the other symbolizes "The Guardian, or Authority, of Law." Huge bronze doors contain sculptured panels depicting historic scenes in the law's development. The courtroom, flanked by 24 Ionic columns, is the principal attraction. The Court hears oral arguments from 10 a.m. to noon and 1 to 3 p.m. from the first Monday in October through the last of April and thereafter sits to hand down opinions through early July.

The Supreme Court is a purely American idea; it has no historic precedent and its role was only vaguely defined in the Constitution. It is basically what its name says it is: the highest, the last Court of the land. The Court consists of eight associate justices and one chief justice appointed by the President with the advice and consent of the Senate. To date the Court has had 16 chief justices, four of whom are pictured above; from left: John Jay, 1789-95; John Marshall, 1801-35; Salmon P. Chase, 1864-73; and William Howard Taft, 1921-30. The Court annually hears arguments on approximately 170 cases out of almost 5,000 petitions submitted. Beginning the first Monday in October the Court hears oral arguments on the cases for three days of each week, alternating every two weeks between hearing cases and being in recess. This does not mean that the Court is not working; quite the contrary, for this is when the justices meet in conference, do research, and write opinions. The work of the Supreme Court has often provided an opposing view to the other two branches of government. At times it has acted as a restraining force on the Executive or the Congress. At other times it has ventured into controversial arenas itself. Always it has acted as the *interpreter* of the Constitution. Like most institutions the Court knows that though individuals may err, a group of persons over time should be able to arrive at solutions beneficial to the greatest number of people. And that is the true test in a democracy.

Folger Shakespeare Library

Neptune Fountain Library of Congress

Alice Paul

④Sewall-Belmont House National Historic Site, 144 Constitution Avenue, NE. Open 10 a.m. to 3 p.m. Tuesday through Friday; noon to 4 p.m. Saturday, Sunday, and holidays. Docents give tours of the house and gardens.

Named for its builder—Robert Sewall—and a benefactress—Alva Belmont—of the National Woman's Party, the house preserves memorabilia of the women's suffrage movement leading to the adoption of the 19th Amendment. Also honored is its most famous resident, Alice Paul, who wrote the proposed equal rights amendment. The house is one of the oldest on Capitol Hill and was declared a national historic site in 1974. Seven restored rooms recapture the Federal period. The National Woman's Party makes its headquarters here.

⑤Folger Shakespeare Library
201 East Capitol Street, SE. The exhibit halls are open 10 a.m. to 4 p.m. The Reading Room, for scholars with permits, is open 8:45 a.m. to 4:45 p.m. Closed holidays. Readers' permits must be obtained in advance from the registrar.

The library contains a premier collection of rare books and manuscripts relating to the Renaissance and the world's largest collection of the works of William Shakespeare. Philanthropist Henry Clay Folger spent his spare time and much of his money acquiring the 7,000 rare books that form the core of the collection, which now numbers about 250,000 volumes and 50,000 manuscripts. It includes an astonishing 66 percent of *all* titles published in English from the invention of printing to 1640.

60

6 Library of Congress, East Capitol and First Streets, SE. The library, consisting of the Thomas Jefferson, John Adams, and James Madison buildings, is open every day except January 1 and December 25. Continuous free guided tours are provided 9 a.m. to 4 p.m. Monday through Friday. The exhibit halls are open 8:30 a.m. to 9:30 p.m. Monday through Friday and 8:30 a.m. to 6 p.m. Saturday and Sunday. For the hours of the reading rooms and reader services, write or call the General Reading Rooms Division.

This institution was established in 1800 as a reference facility for the Congress. That is still one of its most important functions; the Congressional Research Service receives 400,000 requests a year. And at the same time it has grown into one of the great libraries of the world. The original library was lost when the British burned the Capitol in 1814. Thomas Jefferson sold many of his books to the government to reestablish the library, but a second fire destroyed three-fifths of that collection. In 1897 the library moved into the handsome Italian Renaissance structure now named for Jefferson. The mosaics, paintings, and other decorations extol those who have contributed grandly to mankind's knowledge. The John Adams Building was constructed in the late 1930s, and the James Madison Memorial Building was dedicated in 1981. The library, however, is internationally known for its collections, not its architecture. These include one of the largest collections of incunabula (books printed between 1455 and 1501) in the world.

Among the many presidential papers are one of Jefferson's drafts of the Declaration of Independence, Lincoln's drafts of the Gettysburg Address, and Theodore Roosevelt's letters to his children. The American Folklife Center contains recordings of American music collected from the hills and coves of the Southern Appalachians, the Georgia Sea Islands, New Orleans jazz joints, cowboy campfires, and religious gatherings. The Music Division also owns five Stradivari stringed instruments, much operatic literature, and manuscripts of many compositions. During much of the year free evening musical concerts are presented in the Grace Sprague Coolidge Auditorium. At other times, the same room is used for talks or lectures sponsored by the Poetry Office.

61

The Library of Congress owns some of the finest examples of printing and bookmaking known. It owns one of three extant Gutenberg Bibles – the earliest book printed with movable type. It is displayed in the Main Hall just a few steps away from the Great Bible of Mainz, one of the last of the hand-lettered Bibles laboriously produced by scribes in the same city where Gutenberg perfected his invention. The Music Division possesses a large collection of manuscripts by many composers. Here you can find Johannes Brahms' violin concerto, marches by John Philip Sousa, and Rodgers and Hammerstein's working scores and lyrics for *Oklahoma!* Photographs include daguerrotypes made in the earliest days of photography, an extensive Civil War collection, and thousands of pictures taken by WPA photographers in the 1930s. Many miscellaneous, unique treasures can be found in the Library. An example illustrates the breadth of the holdings. In the 1940s one of Abraham Lincoln's granddaughters presented the Library of Congress with a velvet-covered case. Inside were the contents

62

of her grandfather's pockets on the night that he was shot. The only currency in his wallet was a $5 Confederate bill. This photograph, looking into the Main Reading Room, shows a number of items belonging to the Library. From left they are: Leonard Volk's life mask of Lincoln; a violin by Antonio Stradivari; a French Book of Hours, 1524; "Head of Christ" by Anthony Van Dyck; a 1970s facsimile of an 18th-century Chinese scroll, *A City of Cathay;* and a manuscript globe by Caspar Vopell, 1543.

Botanic Garden

Capital Children's Museum

Botanic Garden, Orchids

Capital Children's Museum, activities

7 U.S. Botanic Garden, Maryland Avenue between First and Second Streets, SW. Open 9 a.m. to 5 p.m. daily except January 1 and December 25.

The Botanic Garden was founded in 1820, and the first greenhouse was built in 1842 to house an exotic botanical collection that an expedition led by the explorer Capt. Charles Wilkes brought back from the South Pacific. Construction of the present building began in 1931. Some rooms recreate tropical settings and others depict more arid environments. More than 10,000 plant species from around the world are housed here. Besides sponsoring four special shows annually, the Botanic Garden offers spectacular exhibits, such as its world-renowned collection of orchids. The fountain is by Auguste Bartholdi.

8 Voice of America, 330 Independence Avenue, SW. Tours are given Monday through Friday at 8:40, 9:40, and 10:40 a.m. and 1:40 and 2:40 p.m.

From these studios and newsrooms the United States broadcasts to nations around the world in many languages.

9 Capital Children's Museum, 800 3rd Street, NE. Open 10 a.m. to 5 p.m. daily. Closed January 1, Easter, Thanksgiving, and December 25. Fee.

Hands on is the key to the way this museum operates. Here children, through the pre-teen years, can find their way through the Metamorphomaze, make crafts, and dozens of other things. All are in the spirit of the museum's motto, a Chinese proverb: "I see and I forget. I hear and I remember. I do and I understand."

10 Union Station, Massachusetts and Delaware Avenues, NE. Open 24 hours a day.

The station, modeled on the Baths of Caracalla in Rome, was completed in 1907 as part of revitalization of the National Mall. Until the jet age arrived, visiting dignitaries entered Washington through this station. Today it is a major point for rail travel on the East Coast.

11 National Building Museum, 5th and F Streets, NW. Open 10 a.m. to 4 p.m. Monday through Friday; noon to 4 p.m. Saturday, Sunday, and holidays. Closed Thanksgiving and December 25.

Known for many years as the Old Pension Building, various government offices were housed here from 1883 to 1963. Now, it is dedicated to serving as a museum to buildings and their builders.

64

National Museum of American Art, 8th and G Streets, NW, and the National Portrait Gallery (both Smithsonian Institution), 8th and F Streets, NW. Open 10 a.m. to 5:30 p.m. daily. Closed December 25. Restaurant and museum shop.

The imposing Greek Revival structure that houses these two museums was erected in the mid-1800s halfway between the Capitol and the White House. It became the first home of the Patent Office, and during the Civil War wounded soldiers were treated in its halls. The Smithsonian Institution acquired the building in 1958 and has turned it into these two museums. The National Museum of American Art exhibits outstanding examples of painting, sculpture, graphics, photography, and folk art by American artists.

The subjects range from the lands, waters, and people of the New World through scenes of the growing Nation to those that lend themselves to bold contemporary design. Post World War II paintings and sculpture are shown in the large gallery where Abraham Lincoln's inaugural reception was held. The neighboring National Portrait Gallery is a museum of history seen through the eyes of portrait painters. Responding to Congressional mandate, the gallery has works of Americans noteworthy for contributions to the "history, development and culture" of the people of the United States. Two major portraits, the Gilbert Stuarts of George and Martha Washington, are shared with the Boston Museum of Fine Arts. They alternate three years in Boston and three years here.

National Museum of Women in the Arts, 1250 New York Avenue, NW. Open 10 a.m. to 5 p.m. Tuesday through Saturday; noon to 5 p.m. Sunday.

Opened in 1987, the museum celebrates the achievements of female artists. The collection contains paintings, prints, drawings, sculpture, pottery, and photography from the Renaissance to the present. The museum's goal is to heighten awareness of the contribution of women artists.

65

Ford's Theatre, interior

**Martin Luther King Memorial Library**, 901 G Street, NW. Open 9 a.m. to 9 p.m. Monday through Thursday; 9 a.m. to 5:30 p.m. Friday and Saturday; 1 to 5 p.m. Sunday. Closed holidays.

This is the main building and administrative center for the public libraries of the District of Columbia. This institution is geared to community use rather than to a particular constituency as are many of the great libraries within the city. It is also distinguished by being the only building in Washington designed by architect Ludwig Mies van der Rohe, whose motto was "less is more."

Ford's Theatre, 511 10th Street, NW. **The House Where Lincoln Died**, 516 10th Street, NW. The museum is open 9 a.m. to 5 p.m. daily. Closed December 25. For in-

formation on plays, check the newspapers or call the box office. Open 9 a.m. to 5 p.m. daily. Closed December 25.

The theater has been restored to its appearance on the night of April 14, 1865, when President Abraham Lincoln was shot here by John Wilkes Booth. Among the original items are the sofa in the Presidential box and the framed engraving of George Washington that hung on the front of the box. A museum on the lower level contains exhibits devoted to Lincoln's life and political career. Besides being a museum, Ford's is also an active theater. The National Park Service maintains the building, and the Ford's Theatre Society, a non-profit organization, is responsible for the programs. Over the years the society has turned Ford's into a center for contemporary American

theater, producing plays reflecting our cultural and ethnic diversity.

Across the street is William Petersen's boardinghouse, where Lincoln was taken after he was shot. The President's wife, Mary, and son, Robert, spent the night in the front parlor while in the back parlor Secretary of War Edwin Stanton questioned witnesses. Lincoln died here on the morning of April 15. The furnishings and fixtures of the restored first floor are similar to those that were in the house when Lincoln died.

U.S. Navy Memorial, Pennsylvania Avenue and 8th Street, NW.

Dedicated in 1987, the memorial honors the U.S. Navy. "The Lone Sailor" stands on a gigantic map of the world that focuses on Earth's oceans.

Ford's Theatre, exterior

House Where Lincoln Died

17 Federal Bureau of Investigation, J. Edgar Hoover Building, 10th Street and Pennsylvania Avenue, NW. Tours are free, last one hour, and are given 8:45 a.m. to 4:15 p.m. Monday through Friday. The tour entrance is on E Street. Closed holidays.

In 1975 the FBI moved from the Department of Justice building into this new home. The bureau conducts a tour that includes dramatic presentations of some of its most famous cases, a look at the world-famous FBI laboratory, and a firearms demonstration. Exhibits illustrate past and current investigative activities.

18 The Old Post Office Tower, 1100 Pennsylvania Avenue, NW. Open daily. Tours by glass-enclosed elevator to the tower observation deck are given by the National Park Service 8 a.m. to 11 p.m. April through October; 9 a.m. to 5 p.m. November through March.

For years they said, "Don't tear it down!" Finally the preservationists had their way, and Washington is the richer for this adaptive reuse of the former offices of the Postmaster General. The Pavilion on the ground floor is filled with shops and eateries. The rest of the handsomely restored building now functions as government office space for the National Endowment for the Arts and is named for its first administrator, Nancy Hanks, who was instrumental in saving the building. The Congress Bells, a bicentennial gift from Great Britain, are rung on holidays and special occasions.

19 Freedom Plaza and **Pershing Park,** Pennsylvania Avenue and 14th Street, NW.

This broad flat surface is a nice place to rest between tour stops while you study Pierre L'Enfant's original design for the National Capital that is marked out in colored concrete on the plaza surface. To the west across 14th Street is Pershing Park, an oasis of trees, shrubs, and water in the swirling traffic.

20 Bureau of Engraving and Printing, 14th and C Streets, SW. Continuous tours 8 a.m. to 2 p.m. Monday through Friday. Closed holidays.

This is where they make the money! More than $12 billion worth of U.S. currency is printed here each year. Postage stamps, treasury bonds, and other government securities are printed here.

James Smithson, (1765-1829), was a distinguished English scientist who had never visited the United States. Yet when his nephew died in 1835 without heirs, Smithson's entire fortune of more than $500,000 was left, according to Smithson's stipulation, to the United States "to found at Washington, under the name of the Smithsonian Institution an establishment for the increase and diffusion of knowledge among men." This is all we know about Smithson's hopes and ideals for the institution that would bear his name. But his bequest founded what is today one of the truly great museum complexes in the world. Within its collections the Smithsonian has more than 134 million objects and specimens; only about one percent can be shown at any one time. Among the great national treasures is the 15-star and 15-stripe flag that flew over Baltimore's Fort McHenry during the British bombardment in 1814 and inspired Francis Scott Key to write the "Star-Spangled Banner." In 1909 a descendant of the commanding officer offered it to the Smithsonian, and the restored flag now hangs as the focal point of the Museum of American History. The National Air and Space Museum contains some of the most significant aircraft ever to fly: the Wright brothers' plane, *The Spirit of St. Louis*, a German V2 rocket, and many others. The records and photographs of the Bureau of American Ethnology survive in the National Museum of Natural History's Anthropological Archives. Much of the work of the Smithsonian, however, goes on away from the museums on the Mall. Less well known is the fact that the Smithsonian is a preeminent research institution delving into all aspects of the physical make-up of our planet and the worlds beyond. Major facilities throughout the country and around the world report on geophysical occurrences, astrophysical events, and the quality of marine life and the waters in which they live. A facility of the National Zoo in rural Virginia breeds animals whose survival as a species is dependent on zoos.

Anthropology expeditions search for remains of early humans from Labrador to the South Seas and record vanishing folkways. Most of these ventures have their genesis in the Smithsonian "Castle" (above right), the first of the institution's buildings in Washington. Today the Smithsonian is an organization whose activities relate to the breadth of the human imagination. It has indeed fulfilled the wishes of James Smithson (left).

㉑ Smithsonian Institution, 1000 Jefferson Drive, SW. Open 10 a.m. to 5:30 p.m. daily. Hours for all Smithsonian museums may be extended during the summer. Closed December 25.

When in 1838 the United States received a legacy of more than $500,000 from the estate of James Smithson, Sen. John C. Calhoun thought that the government could not accept it and urged that the fortune be returned. Congressman John Quincy Adams disagreed and worked strenuously for the creation of the Smithsonian Institution. Legislation to authorize it was passed in 1846. The first Smithsonian building, known as "The Castle," was designed by James Renwick and completed in 1855. The original building is now primarily the administrative headquarters, houses the visitor information center, and contains James Smithson's tomb. The institution maintains a variety of remarkable museums in and around Washington. They are: the Anacostia Museum, the Arthur M. Sackler Gallery, the Arts and Industries Building, the Freer Gallery of Art, the Hirshhorn Museum and Sculpture Garden, the National Air and Space Museum, the National Museum of African Art, the National Museum of American Art, the National Museum of American History, the National Museum of Natural History, the National Portrait Gallery, the National Zoo, and the Renwick Gallery. The Smithsonian also administers the Cooper-Hewitt Museum in New York City.

㉒ Freer Gallery of Art (Smithsonian Institution), 12th Street and Jefferson Drive, SW. Closed for construction linking the Freer to the Sackler, 1988 to 1992.

When Charles Freer, a Detroit industrialist, died in 1919, he left behind the foremost collection of Oriental art in North America and more than 100 paintings by James McNeill Whistler. He left this treasure to the United States. He also provided funds to construct a suitable museum and establish an endowment. The gallery exhibits paintings, Oriental porcelains, Japanese screens, painted manuscripts, Persian miniatures and metalwork, and Chinese bronzes dating back to 1100 B.C. Whistler's famous Peacock Room, bought intact by Freer, is a spectacular highlight in this museum of delicate beauty.

㉓ Arthur M. Sackler Gallery (Smithsonian Institution), 1050 Independence Avenue, SW. Open 10 a.m. to 5:30 p.m. daily. Closed December 25. Museum shop.

Chinese bronzes, Near Eastern metalwork and sculptures, and Persian miniatures are on display in this underground museum.

㉔ National Museum of African Art (Smithsonian Institution), 950 Independence Avenue, SW. Open 10 a.m. to 5:30 p.m. daily. Closed December 25. Museum shop.

The Museum of African Art was founded in 1964 to display the cultural heritage of Americans of African descent. The galleries contain displays from the museum's collection of textiles, jewelry, and musical instruments, as well as sculpture in wood, brass, iron, ivory, and gold.

㉕ Arts and Industries Building (Smithsonian Institution), 900 Jefferson Drive, SW. Open 10 a.m. to 5:30 p.m. daily. Closed December 25. Museum shop.

This is the second oldest Smithsonian building on the Mall, erected 1879-80. It was restored to its Victorian appearance when exhibits from the Centennial Exposition were moved to Washington and presented to the Smithsonian. The effect of this gift, which increased the institution's holdings fourfold, was to bring history and technology within the scope of the Smithsonian's activities. Before the exhibits were installed, however, the building was used for President James A. Garfield's inaugural ball in 1881. The exhibits include steam-powered machines as well as lace, telescopes, silverware, perfume, and pistols.

㉖ Hirshhorn Museum and Sculpture Garden (Smithsonian Institution), Independence Avenue and 8th Street, SW. Open 10 a.m. to 5:30 p.m. daily. Closed December 25. Light refreshments are served in the outdoor cafe in warm weather. Museum shop.

Joseph Hirshhorn, an immigrant and self-made millionaire, donated his collection of more than 6,000 paintings and sculptures to the Nation in 1966. A visit here has been called "a capsule course in the history of modern art." The character of the collection is echoed by the circular modern building constructed for it. Although the art includes European creations, the works are primarily American. The Sculpture Garden, across Jefferson Drive, contains the museum's collection of monumental sculpture.

71

National Air and Space Museum, interior from the Mall

National Air and Space Museum, exterior

27 **National Air and Space Museum** (Smithsonian Institution), Independence Avenue from 4th to 7th Streets, SW. Open 10 a.m. to 5:30 p.m. daily. Closed December 25. There is a nomimal charge for presentations in the theater and Spacearium. Food and museum shop.

Opened in 1976, the Air and Space Museum has already become one of the world's most visited museums. It tells the exhilarating story of flight from the Earth's surface through the development of aircraft, rockets, and

spacecraft. The building, not unlike a hangar, has vast interior spaces and lofty ceilings for the proper display of aircraft. All aircraft displayed, and almost all spacecraft, were actually flown. In the Milestones of Flight Gallery hang the plane the Wright brothers first flew at Kitty Hawk in 1903, Charles Lindbergh's *Spirit of Saint Louis*, the X-1 that broke the sound barrier in 1947, the Apollo 11 command module, a moon rock that can be touched, and a full-sized walk-through model of the *Skylab* orbital workshop. Examples of rockets and missiles make a dramatic display. The motion picture theater, with a screen five stories tall, shows films relating to flight. The Albert Einstein Planetarium, a gift of the Federal Republic of Germany, reveals some of the mysteries of the heavens.

28 **National Museum of Natural History and the National Museum of Man** (Smithsonian Institution), 10th Street and Constitution Avenue, NW. Open 10 a.m. to 5:30 p.m. daily. Closed December 25. Cafeteria and museum shop.

The Natural History Museum has two faces: it is a preeminent research institution that explores all facets of life on Earth and beyond, and it is a museum. It is in this latter role that most of us come to know it, for it is a fascinating place to discover the world of plants, animals, fossil organisms, terrestrial and extraterrestrial rocks, and people of this planet. Visitors of all ages find it a treasure house of exhibits that includes the 45.5-carat Hope Diamond, a mounted African bush elephant that stands in the main rotunda, the Star of Asia sapphire, and a life-sized

fiberglass model of a 92-foot-long blue whale. Particular favorites are the Hall of Dinosaurs with its reconstructions of giant prehistoric creatures and the Hall of Mammals in which animals are displayed in settings that reflect their natural surroundings. The Hall of Physical Anthropology shows the development of man from his first emergence on Earth. The Insect Zoo can awaken interest in insects in those who thought they had none. The Splendors of Nature dazzles the eye, while in the Discovery Room you can handle objects and observe them closely. For people with special research interests, the Naturalist Center is available for further study. Some of the finest special exhibits, lasting six months to one year, are to be found in this museum. Ask at the information desk.

㉙ National Museum of American History (Smithsonian Institution), 14th Street and Constitution Avenue, NW. Open 10 a.m. to 5:30 p.m. daily. Closed December 25. Cafeteria and museum shop.

If there is truth to the popular description of the Smithsonian as the "nation's attic," this is the museum that proves it. Here are Eli Whitney's cotton gin, Elias Howe's sewing machine, Thomas Edison's phonograph and light bulb, the flag that inspired Francis Scott Key to write the "Star-Spangled Banner," a Southern Railroad steam engine, Muhammad Ali's boxing gloves, Jackie Robinson's baseball glove, Mr. Roger's sweater, and millions of other items. Much space is devoted to technological development in such fields as photography, printing, transportation, electricity, and the medical

sciences. Exhibits are geared to telling the story of the American experience, letting us know how we have become the Nation we are. Equally important, exhibits focus on our Eastern Hemisphere origins, showing us what our forebears brought with them and what they left behind. In "After the Revolution" visitors can get a glimpse of the newly independent country poised on the brink of the Industrial Revolution. Other exhibits explore the effects of industrialization. Often the exhibits have a hands-on section especially aimed at engaging the imagination and interest of children.

30 **National Archives**, 8th Street and Constitution Avenue, NW. The Exhibition Hall is open 10 a.m. to 5:30 p.m. daily; summer hours may be extended. Closed December 25.

Since the first meeting of the Continental Congress the government has been concerned about keeping records. Preserving them, however, has been difficult. Over the years, they have been burned, ruined by rain and mildew, eaten by insects, sold as junk, and stolen by autograph hunters. Not until 1934 was a proper structure built. The building houses research facilities and displays some of the most vital documents concerning the formation of the United States, including the original copies of the Declaration of Independence, the Constitution, and the Bill of Rights.

31 **National Gallery of Art**, 6th Street and Constitution Avenue, NW. Open 10 a.m. to 5 p.m. Monday through Saturday; noon to 9 p.m. Sunday. Closed January 1 and December 25. The Gallery offers tours, lectures, and films throughout the year, as well as weekly concerts from September through June. Consult the monthly calendar of events for specific information. Cafe, cafeteria, restaurant, and gift shop facilities are located in the buildings.

In half a century the National Gallery has become one of the great art institutions of the world. The works of Rembrandt, Vermeer, Hals, and their compatriots in the Dutch and Flemish schools are well represented, the collection of works by the French impressionists ranks with the best, and the holdings of Italian painting and

sculpture are the most comprehensive in North America. The only painting by Leonardo da Vinci in the Western Hemisphere hangs on the Gallery's walls. The American collection has outstanding works by such masters as John Singleton Copley, Gilbert Stuart, and Rembrandt Peale. The Gallery consists of two buildings: The West, or original, Building and The East Building. They are linked by a plaza and by an underground concourse that houses a bookstore and a cafeteria. The West Building is dominated by the central rotunda with a statue of Mercury, the messenger of the gods, above a fountain. Look for the plaque in the floor near the information desk at the Constitution Avenue entrance that marks the spot where President James Garfield was assassinated

National Gallery of Art, West and East Buildings

when a train station stood at this spot. The West Building was designed by John Russell Pope and built in the late 1930s. The East Building is the work of I.M. Pei and was constructed in the mid-1970s. Both buildings use pink Tennessee marble from the same quarry. There the similarity ends, for each is an expression of its time. The West Building is one of the last structures in the city to bear the stamp of classicism that marks so much of the official architecture. The East Building is one of the city's strongest statements by a contemporary architect.

The National Gallery of Art is essentially a gift to the Nation by the Mellon family. Andrew W. Mellon, secretary of the Treasury for three presidents, 1921–32, assembled one of the most outstanding collections of paintings and sculpture by Old Masters during the early years of the 20th century. While Mellon was ambassador to Great Britain, for example, he bought 21 paintings from the Hermitage in Leningrad. For one of them, Raphael's *Alba Madonna* (above), he paid more than $1 million, an art world record up to that time. In 1937 Mellon presented his collection to the United States along with funds to build the Gallery in which to house them and an endowment. He specifically stated that the build-ing *not* bear his name. Mellon hoped this would encourage other collectors to donate their paintings and sculpture, and it has. The Gallery's West Building opened to the public in 1941 and within 30 years it had been filled through the generous donations from other outstanding art collectors – most notably the Dale, Kress, Widener, and Rosenwald families. More space was needed, and this time Andrew Mellon's son and daughter, Paul Mellon and Ailsa Mellon Bruce, who had already made notable contributions to the collections, provided the funds. The East Building, designed by I.M. Pei, opened to the public in 1978. In its great Central Court hangs one of Alexander Calder's largest mobiles and a tapestry designed by Joan Miró.

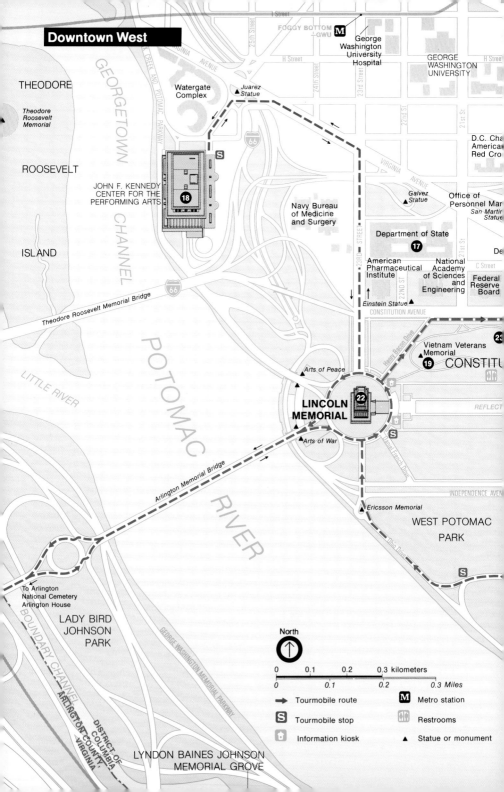

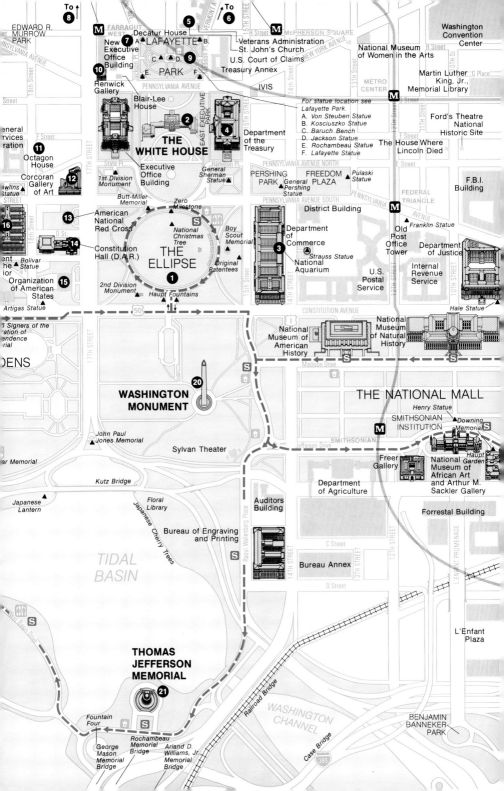

"The President's Own" United States Marine Band, South Portico of the White House

❶ The Ellipse, 1600 Constitution Avenue, NW.

This expanse is used for everything from the annual Christmas Pageant of Peace to ball games and large demonstrations. It contains memorials, two huge fountains each made from a single piece of granite, the zero milestone, and two gatehouses that once stood on the Capitol grounds.

❷ The White House, 1600 Pennsylvania Avenue, NW. Open 10 a.m. to noon Tuesday through Saturday. Closed Sunday, Monday, and some holidays. During the summer free tickets showing the approximate time of the tour are given out at a booth on the Ellipse. These tickets are available on a first-come, first-served basis, and each person must have one. Handicapped persons should go directly to the Northeast Gate on Pennsylvania Avenue for admittance.

The White House has been the official residence of every American President except George Washington. The ground floor contains the great State rooms—East, Green, Blue, and Red Rooms, and the State Dining Room— in which the President entertains his guests. The second floor contains the private rooms reserved for the President and his family. Of the State Rooms, which are open free and regularly to the public (the only residence of a head of state to be readily accessible in the world), the largest is the East Room. It was intended by architect James Hoban to be a "public reception room" and has often served that function. Seven Presidents have lain in

White House, Blue Room

state here. The Gilbert Stuart portrait of George Washington that Dolley Madison saved before the British burned the White House hangs here. Thomas Jefferson used the Green Room as his dining room. Today the furnishings of the room reflect the styles of 1800–15 and most are by New York cabinetmaker Duncan Phyfe. The elliptical Blue Room is decorated in the style first used by James Monroe. Seven of the chairs in the room are the original ones that Monroe ordered from France. The Red Room has generally served as a parlor and does so today. The furniture is of the 1810–30 period, of American manufacture. The State Dining Room can accommodate as many as 140 persons for a formal dinner. Carved into the mantel is John Adams' hope for the White House and its occupants: "I Pray Heaven to Bestow the Best of Blessings on THIS HOUSE and on All that shall hereafter Inhabit it. May none but Honest and Wise Men ever rule under this Roof."

The Residence of the President

The White House was designed by James Hoban, an architect who had been born and raised in Ireland. The house, built of Virginia sandstone painted white, is in the style of an Irish Georgian country house. It is the oldest public building in the District of Columbia, its cornerstone having been laid October 13, 1792, almost one year before a similar ceremony for the Capitol. The White House was barely finished before remodeling began, with practically every subsequent President contributing something. Jefferson, who under a pseudonym had unsuccessfully submitted a design for the residence, added the terraces. Andrew Jackson piped in running water. Franklin Pierce installed a central heating system. Rutherford B. Hayes added the first bathroom and first telephone. The elevator was James A. Garfield's doing. Benjamin Harrison brought in electricity. Herbert Hoover introduced air conditioning. Despite all these alterations, the greatest changes came after the British burned the White House in 1814, when the State Rooms were remodeled in 1902, and during the renovation of 1948–52. Only the walls were left standing after the British burned the structure during their brief occupation of Washington (as shown in the black-and-white engraving of British troops in the city and in the 1816 watercolor with St. John's Church in the foreground). James Hoban, the original architect, supervised the rebuilding, which was completed in September 1817 during James Monroe's administration. In 1902 the architectural firm of McKim, Mead, and White supervised the redecoration and reconditioning of the State floor. During Harry Truman's administration surveys of the structure revealed it to be in an alarming state of disrepair. The Trumans moved across the street to Blair House. Paneling, ceilings, and furniture were all removed and stored. The interior was gutted, a new two-story basement was excavated, new foundations were laid, a steel framework was erected, and everything was put back together again. Previously Truman had added a second story porch to the South Portico. The administrations of John F. Kennedy, Lyndon Johnson, and Richard Nixon concentrated on acquiring antique American furniture for use in the State rooms. During the administrations of Gerald Ford and Jimmy Carter the emphasis turned to finding suitable American paintings and portraits. The arrival of Ronald Reagan signaled an interest in redecorating and refurbishing the family quarters. Heretofore work in this area had been only piecemeal and the efforts begun in the reconstruction of 1948-52 had never been fully realized in the family quarters.

Alone, the words conjure up a host of images. On the one hand the term is almost synonymous with "White House." On the other, it denotes the President at work, functioning as the Chief Executive of the Nation. Here the work of the presidency takes place, here he meets with his advisers, determining policy and courses of action, working out a legislative program, and sometimes speaking to the Nation. Though well known, the term Oval Office is a 20th century creation. Thomas Jefferson used what is now the State Dining Room and James Monroe had an office in the adjacent Treasury building. In John Quincy Adams' administration, the locus of Presidential power was located in a portion of the living quarters on the second floor, and it remained there until the time of Theodore Roosevelt when the demands for more space by the Presidential staff and by the family collided. As a part of the renovation of the main floor that Roosevelt initiated, a "temporary" structure—the West Wing—was erected to contain offices for his staff.

An office for the President was located here, but he seldom used it. Seven years later the temporary building was reconstructed as a permanent office and the term "Oval Office" dates from this time. On Christmas Eve 1929 a fire destroyed most of the structure; it was rebuilt the next year. In 1934 the West Wing was greatly enlarged to meet the need for the even larger staff that President Franklin D. Roosevelt assembled. With some small changes this is the West Wing and Oval Office in use today. Many Presidents, including Ronald Reagan, have chosen to use the desk that Queen Victoria presented to Rutherford B. Hayes. It is made from the timbers of HMS *Resolute*, a British ship rescued from the pack ice of the Arctic Ocean by the American whalers (shown in a contemporary engraving).

Alexander Hamilton, U.S. Treasury

St. John's Church

❸ The National Aquarium, U.S. Department of Commerce, 14th Street and Pennsylvania Avenue, NW. Open 9 a.m. to 5 p.m. daily. Closed December 25. Fee, gift shop.

They feed the piranhas and lemon sharks on alternate days at 2 p.m. The sea turtles waddle at eye level and children can discover the feel of starfish, crabs, and other sea animals in the Touch Tank.

❹ Department of the Treasury, 15th Street and Pennsylvania Avenue, NW.

The Treasury building is one of the finest examples of Greek Revival architecture in America. A statue of Alexander Hamilton, the first secretary of the Treasury, stands on the south plaza, and one of Albert Gallatin, the fourth secretary, on the north. No public facilities.

❺ St. John's Church, 16th and H Streets, NW. Open 7 a.m. to 7 p.m. daily. Tours are given every Sunday after the 11 a.m. service.

St. John's was designed by Benjamin Latrobe and built in 1816. Most Presidents have at times attended services. President John F. Kennedy, a Roman Catholic, once visited the rector to continue the tradition. The bell in the steeple was recast in Paul Revere's foundry from a captured British cannon. One stained glass window is a gift from President Chester Arthur in memory of his wife who had been a member of the choir. Arthur asked that the window be placed so he could see it from the White House as the light shone through it at night. The parish house was once the British ambassador's residence.

❻ Mary McLeod Bethune Council House, 1318 Vermont Avenue, NW. Open 10 a.m. to 4:30 p.m. Monday through Friday; Saturday, Sunday, and holidays by appointment.

The museum is dedicated to the lives and achievements of black American women. The restored Victorian townhouse was declared a national historic site in 1982 in honor of the pioneer black political and civil rights leader and educator. Bethune, who founded the National Council of Negro Women, resided here and made this the headquarters of the council. Housed here are the National Archives for Black Women's History. The museum organizes tours and special programs for schoolchildren and also serves teachers and scholars. The house is a stop on the Washington, D.C., Black History Trail.

Bethune Council House

7 Decatur House, 748 Jackson Place, NW. Open 10 a.m. to 2 p.m. Tuesday through Friday; noon to 4 p.m. Saturday and Sunday. Closed Monday and holidays. Tours are given every half hour. Fee.

This impressive townhouse, designed by Benjamin Latrobe, was completed in 1819 for Commodore Stephen Decatur, a naval hero of the Barbary Wars and the War of 1812. It is an excellent example of a Federal style residence and adds to the beauty of Lafayette Park. Decatur died here after being mortally wounded in a duel with Capt. James Barron in 1820. Since that time a number of famous people have lived here, including Henry Clay, Martin Van Buren, and Judah P. Benjamin. The National Trust for Historic Preservation has owned the property since 1956.

8 The National Geographic Society/Explorers Hall, 17th and M Streets, NW. Open 9 a.m. to 5 p.m. Monday through Saturday and holidays; 10 a.m. to 5 p.m. on Sunday. Closed December 25.

The headquarters of the National Geographic Society contains a museum that illustrates some of the society's worldwide interests. The fascinating history of our planet—its physical make-up, the efforts of humans to explore it, and the diverse cultures of its peoples—is told through photographs, videos, and dioramas.

89

Renwick Gallery, Grand Salon

The Octagon, Treaty of Ghent desk

❾ Lafayette Park, directly north of the White House.

In the center of the park is a statue of Andrew Jackson made from cannon he captured during the War of 1812. At the corners of the park are statues of Thaddeus Kosciuszko, baron von Steuben, the comte de Rochambeau, and the marquis de Lafayette. The bench where Bernard Baruch, adviser to Presidents, sat is also marked.

❿ Renwick Gallery (Smithsonian Institution), Pennsylvania Avenue at 17th Street, NW. Open 10 a.m. to 5:30 p.m. daily. Closed December 25. Museum shop.

This gallery exhibits American crafts, dating from 1900 to the present. A room of great size on the second floor recreates an elegant Victorian Grand Salon of the 1860s and 1870s. Originally this building was the Corcoran Gallery of Art designed in 1859 by architect James Renwick, who had earlier drawn up the plans for the Smithsonian Institution. Before Corcoran could open his museum, Civil War intervened and the building became the headquarters of the quartermaster general. Finally in 1871 the Corcoran opened its doors to its first visitors; the museum was a success. By the 1890s the Corcoran needed more facilities and moved to its new building in 1897. From 1899 to 1964 the building housed the U.S. Court of Claims. In 1972, renamed for its architect, it opened as one of the Smithsonian museums.

⓫ The Octagon, 1799 New York Avenue, NW. Open 10 a.m. to 4 p.m. Tuesday through Friday; noon to 4 p.m. Saturday and Sunday. Closed Mondays and major holidays. Fee.

When Col. John Tayloe, III, decided to build a new home in Washington, he selected Dr. William Thornton to create a design for him. The Tayloes called it the Octagon because of the eight angles in the plan. James and Dolley Madison lived here for a short time after the British burned the White House in 1814. In the second floor study is the desk upon which President Madison signed the Treaty of Ghent. The American Architectural Foundation bought the house from the Tayloe family in 1902 and has since maintained it as a museum.

The Octagon

Corcoran Gallery of Art

⓬ Corcoran Gallery of Art, 17th Street and New York Avenue, NW. Open 10 a.m. to 4:30 p.m. Tuesday through Sunday; Thursday until 9 p.m. Closed holidays. The gallery maintains an extensive program of tours and lectures as well as chamber music.

The Corcoran is especially noted for its collection of American art. It is also one of the oldest art museums in the country, having been incorporated the same year—1870—as New York City's Metropolitan Museum of Art and the Boston Museum of Fine Arts. On display are works by John Singleton Copley, Gilbert Stuart, the Peales, Thomas Cole, Thomas Eakins, Mary Cassatt, Albert Bierstadt, and Frederic Remington. Changing exhibits display works of contemporary artists and photographers.

⓭ The American National Red Cross, 17th and E Streets, NW. Open 8:30 a.m. to 4:45 p.m. Monday through Friday. Closed weekends and holidays.

The national headquarters of the Red Cross has exhibit areas on the ground and main floors. The Board of Governors Hall has three Tiffany windows.

⓮ Daughters of the American Revolution National Society Headquarters, 1776 D Street, NW. Open 8:30 a.m. to 4 p.m. Monday through Friday; 1 to 5 p.m. on Sunday. Tours of the period rooms 10 a.m. to 2:30 p.m. Monday through Friday. Library open 9 a.m. to 4 p.m. Monday through Friday; fee for use.

This is the headquarters for descendants of Revolutionary War veterans. The library has an outstanding genealogical collection; it is open to the public except for most of the month of April when it is reserved for members.

⓯ Organization of American States, 17th Street at Constitution Avenue, NW. Open 9 a.m. to 4 p.m. Monday through Friday. Closed Saturday, Sunday, and holidays. Group tours may be arranged by calling 458-3751 or by writing to the Visitors Service Unit, Department of Public Information.

Aztec, Mayan, and Inca motifs skillfully blended with European influences create a structure that represents both Americas. In the Hall of the Americas many international meetings and musical recitals have been held.

91

Department of State

John F. Kennedy Center for the Performing Arts

⑯ U.S. Department of the Interior, 18th and C Streets, NW. The museum is open 8 a.m. to 4 p.m.; the Indian Craft Shop is open 8:30 a.m. to 4:30 p.m.; and National Park Service Information is open 9 a.m. to 5 p.m.; all Monday through Friday. Closed weekends and holidays.

Through displays on national parks, Native American pottery and basketry, water power, wildlife, mineralogy, and cartography, Interior presents its manifold activities in the department's museum on the first floor of its headquarters building. In the corridors of this large office building are murals, frescoes, relief sculptures in stone, and paintings—some of the finest Depression-era public art in the country.

⑰ U.S. Department of State, 2201 C Street, NW. When not being used for official functions, the diplomatic reception rooms are open for tours by reservation, Monday through Friday. For information contact the Tour Office, 647-3421.

Within this mid-20th century office building, the floor that houses the diplomatic reception rooms is very much in the style of the 18th and early 19th centuries. The rooms are filled with rare examples of the finest American furniture, paintings, lighting fixtures, and the decorative arts. The desk at which John Adams, Benjamin Franklin, and John Jay signed the Treaty of Paris for the United States is in the John Quincy Adams State Drawing Room along with Benjamin West's painting depicting the event.

⑱ The John F. Kennedy Center for the Performing Arts, 2700 F Street, NW. Open 10 a.m. to 9 p.m. daily. Box office open 10 a.m. to 9 p.m. Monday through Saturday; noon to 9 p.m. Sunday and holidays. Tours of the theaters lasting 40 minutes are given 10 a.m. to 1 p.m. daily by the Friends of the Kennedy Center. Parking is on three lower levels with free parking for people buying or picking up tickets.

More than 200 years ago President George Washington urged that a national cultural center be planned for the new national capital. In 1958 President Dwight D. Eisenhower signed legislation authorizing its establishment. In the outpouring of grief and affection after President John Kennedy's assassination in 1963, the center was named in his memory. Some funds

Three Servicemen's Statue, Vietnam Veterans Memorial
© F.E. Hart and VVMF, Inc., 1984

were appropriated for construction and work got underway in 1966. The center opened officially on September 8, 1977, and performances have been staged ever since. The Center contains the Eisenhower Theater for plays and dramatic performances; the Opera House for ballet, opera, and musical theater; the Concert Hall for musical performances; the American Film Institute Theater for screening movies; and the Terrace Theater for chamber music and small dance, dramatic productions, or concert presentations.

⓳ Vietnam Veterans Memorial, Constitution Gardens, NW. Open 24 hours a day.

The Vietnam Veterans Fund was incorporated April 27, 1979, to establish a memorial to those men and women who served and died during the Vietnam War. The members of the Fund wished to create a memorial that would be contemplative in character, that would harmonize with its surroundings, that would contain the names of all who died or remain missing, and that would make no political statement about the war. Money was raised from private groups and individuals to finance the design and construction of the memorial; no public funds were used. The design competition was won by Maya Ying Lin, who in 1981 was an architecture student at Yale University. The memorial is built of polished black granite set into the ground in the form of a "V" with one arm pointing toward the Lincoln Memorial and the other toward the Washington Monument. The names are in the chronological order of the date of the casualty from the first deaths in 1959 until the last ones in 1975. Altogether 58,156 names are inscribed on the memorial's walls. A statuary group of three young soldiers by sculptor Frederick Hart stands at the entry to the memorial. The memorial was dedicated November 13, 1982. It has become one of the most visited spots in Washington.

93

The Vietnam War made an indelible impression on most Americans 15 years or older in 1965 whether or not they were directly involved in the war. As days, weeks, months, and years have gone by since the war ended, people have begun to look back at those times, trying to make sense of what went on and trying to live with the legacy that survives. The Vietnam Veterans Memorial, on the Mall between the Lincoln Memorial and Constitution Gardens, has been a focal point of this reconciliation process as we mourn the loss of young men and women and attempt to comprehend what this loss has meant for the future of our Nation. Family members, friends, and acquaintances make the pilgrimage to find the name of a loved one carved onto this wall. Many take rubbings of the name on a piece of paper to take home with them. They leave notes, pictures, snapshots, flowers, a childhood toy, a high school reunion program – all mementos of either family life or friendship. And those who know no one whose name appears on this wall come, too, to remember those times that affected us all, and to come to terms with their emotions as well. The volunteers who work here assisting the National Park Service have become the living embodiment of this reconciliation process. By helping people locate a name and by providing information about the memorial itself, they bring the memorial and people together as citizens from across the Nation come at all hours of the day to pay their respects to those who lost their lives in this war. The

effect of seeing a name you know and of seeing all the names is powerful beyond expectation. The process of healing so hoped for by the people who planned this memorial has taken firm root here.

⑳ The Washington Monument, 15th Street and Constitution Avenue, NW. Open 9 a.m. to 5 p.m. daily with extended summer hours for splendid nighttime views of the city. Elevator is the only way up or down. Walking tours down the steps to see the memorial stones are given at 10 a.m. and 3 p.m., staff permitting. On the monument grounds is the Sylvan Theater, an open-air stage used for theatrical productions.

Proposals for honoring George Washington were made with growing regularity

after his death in 1799. L'Enfant had included plans for an equestrian statue of Washington at the intersection of the Capitol's east-west axis and the White House's north-south axis as a part of his design, but Washington had rejected it. The idea surfaced in 1816, 1819, 1824, 1825, and 1832, the centennial of his birth. The collapse of the 1832 proposal led George Watterston, the Librarian of Congress, to found the Washington National Monument Society to raise money and construct the me-

morial. A competition for a design was won by Robert Mills, whose plan called for a shaft 600 feet high surrounded at its base by a circular building that was to serve as a national pantheon containing statues of notable figures in American history. Atop the door Mills planned to install a huge figure of Washington driving a chariot. Meanwhile the fund-raising lagged, and Congress balked at providing federal land. In 1848, however, these problems were resolved and ground was broken. Work had proceeded to

the 152-foot level by 1854, when the "Know Nothings," an anti-Catholic, anti-foreign political party seized the monument because Pope Pius IX had sent a block of marble from Rome's Temple of Concord to be set into the interior wall with other memorial stones from foreign, state, and local governments and private organizations. The papal stone disappeared, and work on the monument also stopped. Work resumed in 1876 and proceeded at a good pace. The monument was dedicated February 21, 1885, with Robert Winthrop, who had spoken at the laying of the cornerstone 40 years earlier, giving the address. It was opened October 9, 1888. As it stands today the Washington Monument is a hollow obelisk, a four-sided pillar that tapers as it rises 555 feet and ends in a pyramid. It is one of the largest masonry structures in the world. Most of the stone is from Maryland. When work resumed on the monument in 1876, marble from the Maryland quarry could not be obtained, so matching marble was found in Massachusetts and laid for 13 courses. The Maryland marble again became available and was used to finish off the remainder of the monument. The new marble, however, has weathered to a slightly different shade, making it easy to see the two different stages of construction. The top of the monument is a 100-ounce cap of aluminum, the largest piece cast to that time.

Thomas Jefferson Memorial, cherry trees in full bloom

㉑Thomas Jefferson Memorial, East Basin Drive, SW. Open daily 8 a.m. to midnight.

In 1934 Congress created the Thomas Jefferson Memorial Commission to find a location, develop a design, and supervise the construction of a memorial to the third President in the Nation's Capital. Despite its high-minded goal, the commission encountered challenges at almost every step along the way. Today the site on the Tidal Basin, south of the White House, seems inspired, but it was arrived at only after the rejection of proposed locations on the Mall, in Lincoln Park, and on the banks of the Anacostia River. Disagreements about the design of the memorial erupted immediately. Other opposition arose because some cherry trees had to be removed before construction could begin. On December 15, 1938, President Franklin D. Roosevelt participated in the groundbreaking ceremony, and one year later the cornerstone was laid. On Jefferson's 200th birthday, April 13, 1943, the memorial was dedicated. Because of the scarcity of metal in the midst of World War II, the statue of Jefferson was first made of plaster; it was replaced with a bronze statue, as originally specified, on April 25, 1947. The Jefferson memorial reflects the essence of the man whom it honors. The graceful, domed building is the architectural shape Jefferson used in desiging his own home, Monticello, and the University of Virginia. The memorial design is by John Russell Pope whose work in Washington includes the National Archives and the

National Gallery of Art, West Building. Pope died before construction began and the final design work was done by Otto Eggers and Daniel Higgins. The heroic statue was sculpted by Rudulph Evans. Inscribed on four panels along the interior walls are selections from Jefferson's writings on liberty. The first panel contains excerpts from the Declaration of Independence. The second is from his Virginia Statute of Religious Freedom. The third is about slavery and the fourth about the need for accepting change in a democracy. The beauty of the memorial on the banks of the Tidal Basin is heightened each spring when the Japanese cherry trees bloom. In 1909 Mrs. William Howard Taft became interested in planting Japanese cherries in Potomac Park. Through the efforts of Dr. Jokichi Takamine, the discoverer of adrenalin, the City of Tokyo presented some 3,000 flowering cherry trees to the City of Washington. The first two trees were planted by Mrs. Taft and Viscountess Chinda, wife of the Japanese ambassador, on March 27, 1912. Also on the grounds are a Japanese lantern more than 300 years old and a pagoda, both given by the Japanese in honor of Commodore Matthew Perry's mission to Japan in 1854. In recent years, older trees that die have been replaced with donations from individual and corporate patrons.

㉒ Lincoln Memorial, foot of 23rd Street, NW. The memorial is always open and a Park Service ranger is on duty 8 a.m. to midnight daily, except December 25.

There never was any question that there should be a memorial to Lincoln, but where to put it, and what it should be were questions that caused much debate. The present location at the west end of the Mall, balancing the Capitol on the east, seems logical today, but at the turn of the century the site was a swampy wasteland. The in-

fant automobile industry pushed for a federal highway from Washington, D.C., to Gettysburg, Pennsylvania, lined with statues and commemorative structures erected by the states. In 1911, the Lincoln Memorial Commission chaired by President William Howard Taft began work. For a site, the commission chose West Potomac Park, which had been drained and reclaimed from the Potomac River. Shortly afterwards the commission decided upon Henry Bacon as the architect. The cornerstone was laid

February 12, 1915. As work on the foundation proceeded, the commissioners searched for a sculptor and eventually agreed upon Daniel Chester French. French wrestled with the problem of how to present the figure of Lincoln. Should it be a standing figure, and, if so, what pose would be best? Or would a seated figure be more appropriate to the structure? Finally French settled on a seated figure brooding over the burdens of the Civil War. The original specifications called for a 10-foot-high fig-

ure, but French soon realized that a statue that size would be dwarfed in Bacon's temple. Doubling the figure solved the problem. The Lincoln Memorial's classic white marble structure is designed in the style of a Greek temple but with its entrance on the east side instead of at either end. Carved on the walls are the Gettysburg Address and Lincoln's Second Inaugural. The 36 marble columns represent the States of the Union at the time of Lincoln's death, and the names of these states are carved on the frieze above the columns. The names of the 48 states in the Union when the memorial was completed in 1922 are carved on the walls above the frieze. A plaque honoring the subsequent entry of Alaska and Hawaii is in the approach plaza. On the day of dedication, May 30, 1922, more than 50,000 people arrived for the ceremonies. Among the notables was Robert Todd Lincoln, the only surviving son of the President. Since that day the memorial has become a national forum—the setting for celebrations, for the airing of grievances, and for commemorations.

㉓Constitution Gardens, Constitution Avenue and 17th Street, NW.

On the north side of the Lincoln Memorial reflecting pool, landscaped gardens, meandering footpaths, and a lake have replaced temporary office buildings that stood here for almost 50 years. On an island in the lake is a memorial to the Signers of the Declaration of Independence.

When Pierre L'Enfant drew up his plan for Washington (see pages 50-51), the Potomac shoreline roughly followed Constitution Avenue, 17th Street, and Maine Avenue, so his design stopped at the river's edge. Beyond were marshes and tidal mudflats that were awash at high tide (as is indicated in the 1855 pen and ink drawing showing the unfinished Washington Monument with the Smithsonian Building and the Capitol in the distance and a fisherman in the foreground). For years little attention was

paid to L'Enfant's Plan, and it was honored more by inaction than by direction. The swamps and marshes sat there for years, almost in the heart of the city. Finally in 1881 Congress appropriated money to dredge out the Potomac and use the muck brought up from the river's bottom to fill the marshes and mudflats and raise them above the high tide line. By the time this project ended around the turn of the century, both West and East Potomac Parks had been created, the Washington Channel and the Potomac had been

dredged to a depth that would allow boats to moor at the foot of Maine Avenue, and the Tidal Basin had been constructed so as to keep the water in the channel from becoming stagnant. In 1911 a site in West Potomac Park in line with the Capitol was selected for the Lincoln Memorial. As this new land was created the initial idea was that it would simply be a westward extension of the Mall's greensward. The ideal was a long time in being achieved, for during World Wars I and II "temporary"

office buildings were erected on these new lands for the business of running a government in wartime. Not until the mid-1970s did the last of these temporary structures come down. Then President Richard Nixon proposed that the area be developed as Constitution Gardens (shown here) in honor of the Nation's bicentennial. Today from the steps of the Capitol to the shores of the Potomac at the foot of the Lincoln Memorial almost two miles away, the Mall sweeps in the grand style L'Enfant envisioned.

The downtown and Mall are the Washington that we all know about, and it is the one that most of us come to see. But, beyond this monumental core lies an area rich with exciting museums, historic homes, Civil War battlefields, lovely gardens, ethereal churches, parks for children, and natural wonders. In the following pages you no doubt will find something to tantalize you and amplify your trip to Washington.

The sites listed here are in the District of Columbia and in nearby Virginia and Maryland and keyed to the map at left. Many of these sites can be reached by public transportation, but almost as many are accessible only by private vehicle. While you travel from one site to another, keep an eye on the landscape, for the Washington area lies across the fall line, that point at which interior rivers fall to sea level along the East Coast. Thus parts of the area—to the south and east—lie in the flat coastal plain while the rest is in the rolling Piedmont.

Development has overwhelmed several historic towns, but if you look hard enough you can usually find signs of their roots. Street and road names, too, give clues to their past: Little River Turnpike and Jones Mill Road to mention just two. And if you get lost, do not despair. Area residents are conscious that this city belongs to the entire Nation and will try to send you off in the right direction, unless they themselves are among the many newcomers who are just learning their way around, too.

Beyond Downtown

1 Anacostia Museum
2 Armed Forces Medical Museum
3 Chesapeake and Ohio Canal National Historical Park
4 Columbia Historical Society
5 Dumbarton Oaks
6 Fort Dupont Park
7 Frederick Douglass NHS

8 Georgetown
9 Hillwood
10 The Islamic Center
11 Kenilworth Aquatic Gardens
12 The National Shrine of the Immaculate Conception
13 National Zoological Park
14 Naval Observatory
15 Navy Memorial Museum

16 Old Stone House
17 The Phillips Collection
18 Rock Creek Park
19 The Textile Museum
20 U.S. National Arboretum
21 Washington Cathedral
22 The Washington Post
23 Woodrow Wilson House

Nearby Maryland

24 Clara Barton National Historic Site
25 Fort Washington
26 Glen Echo Park
27 Great Falls Tavern

28 Greenbelt Park
29 National Aeronautics and Space Administration
30 National Capital Trolley Museum

31 Oxon Hill Farm
32 Piscataway Park and the National Colonial Farm

Nearby Virginia

33 Alexandria
34 Arlington House
35 Arlington National Cemetery
36 The Athenaeum
37 Carlyle House
38 Claude Moore Colonial Farm
39 Friendship Fire Engine Company
40 George Washington Memorial Parkway
41 George Washington Masonic National Memorial
42 Great Falls Park
43 Gunston Hall Plantation

44 Lee-Fendall House
45 The Lyceum
46 Lyndon Baines Johnson Memorial Grove on the Potomac
47 Manassas National Battlefield Park
48 Mount Vernon
49 The Pentagon
50 Prince William Forest Park
51 Boyhood Home of Robert E. Lee
52 Stabler Leadbeater Apothecary Shop
53 Theodore Roosevelt Island

54 U.S. Marine Corps War Memorial and the Netherlands Carillon
55 Washington's Grist Mill Historical State Park
56 Wolf Trap Farm Park
57 Woodlawn Plantation and the Pope-Leighey House

C&O Canal (left) and
Dumbarton Oaks (below)

Nearly everyone is familiar with the great national memorials; they are the images that come to mind when someone talks about going to Washington. But away from this monumental core exists a normal, middle-sized, American city of neighborhoods, private museums, places of worship, shops and stores, restaurants, and schools. Some of the places described on the following pages evoke a sense of Washington as a city of more than 650,000 people who share the aspirations and dreams of their fellow citizens across the Nation. These places are just suggestions of what can be found throughout the city. Some of the places mentioned are stops on the Black History Trail that weaves through the city linking a number of sites important to the history of black Americans. The Civil War forts that ringed the city can be found in varying states of preservation in the Fort Circle Parks. Other sites will give you a glimpse into special collections, architecturally significant structures, and historic places that have much to offer. Without doubt your explorations will introduce you to much that will delight you beyond these sites, whether it is enjoying a meal at a small cafe, or lazing away a few hours.

① **Anacostia Museum** (Smithsonian Institution), 1901 Fort Place, SE. Open 10 a.m. to 5 p.m. daily. Closed December 25.

The museum, located in the historic Anacostia section of Southeast Washington, presents exhibits on the history and culture of Afro-Americans.

② **Armed Forces Medical Museum**, 14th and Dahlia Streets, NW (Walter Reed Army Medical Center). Open 9:30 a.m. to 4:30 p.m. Monday through Friday and 11:30 a.m. to 4:30 p.m. Saturday, Sunday, and holidays. Closed January 1, Thanksgiving, December 24, 25, and 31.

The museum opened in 1862 and has many historical artifacts and anatomical specimens. Current exhibits focus on public health problems, such as AIDS.

③ Chesapeake and Ohio Canal National Historical Park, ticket office on first floor of the Foundry Building on the canal between 30th and Thomas Jefferson Streets, NW. Open Wednesday through Sunday mid-April through mid-October.

In season, boat trips of varying lengths leave from lock 2 at the Foundry Building. Check there for detailed information.

④ Columbia Historical Society, 1307 New Hampshire Avenue, NW. Library open 10 a.m. to 4 p.m. Wednesday, Friday, and Saturday. Tours noon to 4 p.m. Wednesday through Saturday. Closed Sundays, Mondays, and holidays.

The society has programs and a library on the history of the District of Columbia. The building is the former mansion of Christian Heurich, who made a fortune brewing beer in Washington.

⑤ Dumbarton Oaks, 1703 32nd Street, NW. Open 2 to 5 p.m. Tuesday through Sunday. Closed holidays. Museum shop. Fee for visiting the gardens only.

Situated at the edge of Georgetown and named for the Rock of Dumbarton in Scotland, this estate most recently belonged to Mr. and Mrs. Robert Woods Bliss who left it to Harvard University. It is now a research center dedicated to Byzantine studies. This was the site of the conference that laid the groundwork for the United Nations. Visitors may walk through a series of landscaped gardens of remarkable variety and charm. A small gallery displays a collection of pre-Columbian treasures.

⑥ Fort Dupont Park, Minnesota and Massachusetts Avenue, SE. Open daily.

This is the site of one of Washington's Civil War forts. Today it is an expansive playground with tennis and basketball courts, softball fields, and other playing fields. There are biking and hiking trails, picnic areas, and other recreational facilities. The Activity Center has a wide variety of programs. To find the remains of the Civil War fort for which this park is named, follow the path from the parking lot at the Fort Dupont Activity Center. Signs will direct you to the remains of the earthworks that sit atop a ridge. The original fort was six-sided, each side 100 feet long.

107

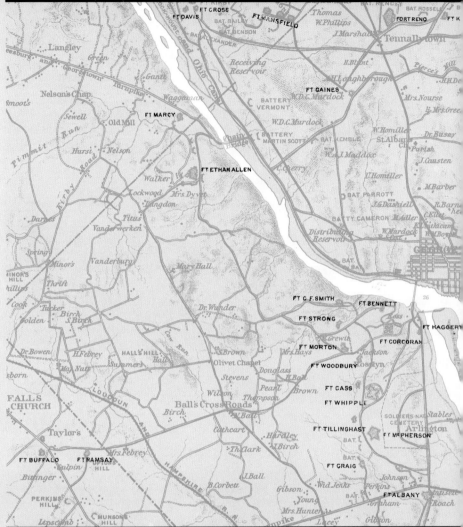

Washington, D.C., was in a precarious position when the Civil War began in 1861. Technically Virginia, across the river, was a foreign country, and many Marylanders, to the north, east, and west of the city, favored secession. Southerners looked upon the city as a prize whose capture might guarantee independence for the Confederacy. Northerners regarded the city as the symbol of national authority and supremacy that had to be defended. Fort Washington, 12 miles down the Potomac opposite Mount Vernon, was the sole fortification guarding the city in 1861, and it was decrepit and outmoded. By the time the war ended four years later a ring of 68 forts and 93 batteries with 837 guns surrounded the city and guarded its approaches. In July 1864, troops from Fort Stevens stopped Confederate troops that were riding into the District of Columbia near today's Georgia Avenue and Somerset Place, NW, in a battle watched by President Lincoln. No other fort saw action during the war. Today these forts and batteries are all being maintained as park areas. Any historic remains are being preserved. Some are used as play

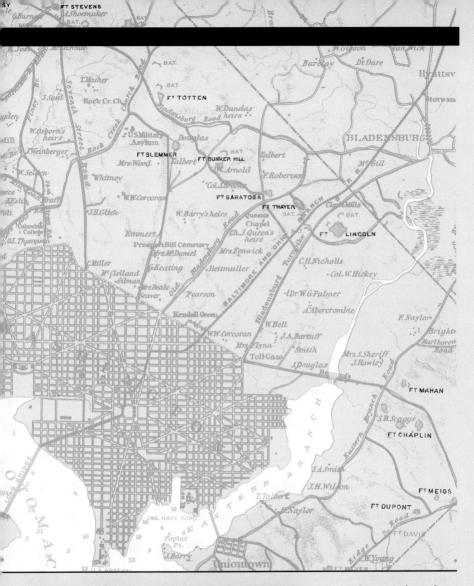

areas, others remain as plots of green amidst the urban sprawl. Many forts still retain a hint of their original shape through vague grassy outlines on the ground. A few, such as Fort Stevens and Fort Foote (left), have been partially rebuilt. Collectively they are known as the Fort Circle Parks and are administered by National Capital Region of the National Park Service.

109

Frederick Douglass' Study

A street in Georgetown

7 Frederick Douglass National Historic Site, 1411 W Street, SE. Open 9 a.m. to 4 p.m. daily. Closed January 1 and December 25.

Frederick Douglass was born a slave either in 1817 or 1818 in Talbot County, Maryland. He escaped bondage in 1838 and went on to become one of the most eloquent leaders of the abolitionist movement. After the struggle for emancipation was finally won, Douglass continued his fight for equal rights and held high positions in the Federal Government. He eventually settled in this handsome house with a commanding view of the city. The house is maintained by the National Park Service as a museum to his memory and contains many interesting artifacts of his life, including his comprehensive library.

8 Georgetown, centered on M Street and Wisconsin Avenue, NW.

Originally Georgetown was one of three cities—the others were Alexandria and Washington—within the District of Columbia. In 1871, it was incorporated into the city of Washington. Today Georgetown is a community of beautiful 18th- and 19th-century townhouses. Wisconsin Avenue and M Street are the main commercial streets. The surrounding tree-lined streets are ideal for leisurely walking tours. Anywhere you choose to walk will be rewarding, for the structures illustrate the wide range of architecture popular in Washington throughout the years. Local bookstores carry guides to the area, some of which contain suggested walking tours and detailed information about the area.

9 Hillwood, 4155 Linnean Avenue, NW. A limited number of two-hour tours are given every day except Tuesday and Sunday. Reservations are required; call 686-5807. Fee.

Hillwood was the home of Marjorie Merriweather Post, the heiress to the General Foods fortune and promoter of frozen foods. Hillwood sits amidst azaleas, rhododendrons, and dogwoods whose blooms burst forth in the Washington springtime, a delight to the eye.

10 The Islamic Center, 2551 Massachusetts Avenue, NW. Open 10 a.m. to 5 p.m. daily. Proper dress is required when entering: arms and legs must be covered and shoes must be removed.

The interior of the mosque, a center for worship and learning, is a treasury of Islamic artwork.

Kenilworth Aquatic Gardens

The National Shrine

Islamic Center

11 Kenilworth Aquatic Gardens, Anacostia Avenue and Douglass Street, NE. Open daily. Closed December 25 and January 1. Picnic tables are available. National Park Service naturalists conduct nature walks in the gardens on summer weekends.

In 1882 W.B. Shaw planted some water lilies from his home in Maine at his new home on the Anacostia River. This inauspicious event was the beginning of a vast enterprise. Today's garden includes specimens from around the world. The ponds, marshes, and the Anacostia estuary provide habitats for waterfowl and small mammals. The display is particularly striking in mid-June when some 70 varieties of day-blooming lilies are at their peak, and again in July and August when the day- and night-blooming varieties open.

12 The National Shrine of the Immaculate Conception, 4th Street and Michigan Avenue, NE. Open daily; tours throughout the day.

This is the largest Roman Catholic church in the United States and the seventh largest church in the world. The shrine is both massive in size and rich in detail. The tower houses a 56-bell carillon. The shrine has chapels scattered throughout. The upper church is marked by towering walls, while the crypt captures the spirit of the Roman catacombs. Among the shrine's treasures are three magnificent mosaics: "Christ in Majesty," in the north apse, and reproductions of Murillo's "Immaculate Conception," and Titian's "Assumption of the Virgin." The latter two mosaics were gifts to the United States from Vatican City.

Pandas in the National Zoo

A summer day at the Zoo

Orangutan

⓭ National Zoological Park (Smithsonian Institution), 3000 Connecticut Avenue, NW. Open daily. May 1 through September 15: grounds 8 a.m. to 8 p.m.; animal houses 9 a.m. to 6 p.m. September 16 through April 30: grounds 8 a.m. to 6 p.m.; animal houses 9 a.m. to 4:30 p.m. Closed December 25.

The Zoo was established by Congress in 1889 when a collection of North American animals housed behind the Smithsonian "Castle" on the Mall was moved to the wooded slopes of Rock Creek valley. Enhanced by special expeditions, gifts, and exchanges, the collection now contains approximately 4,000 animals representing about 500 species from around the world. Included are the famous giant pandas from China, a magnificent white tiger from India, and Aldabra tortoises. For many years Smokey the Bear, the symbol of forest fire prevention, was the Zoo's most famous inhabitant. Today his successor resides here. Such familiar animals as sea lions, monkeys, elephants, and a variety of reptiles are represented as well as such exotic creatures as scimitar-horned oryxes, golden lion tamarins, African bongos, and Galapagos tortoises. There is a spectacular birdhouse where the birds fly freely in a walk-through outdoor cage. Recent renovations have been carried out with emphasis on enclosures that resemble natural habitats. Besides its role as a place where people go to see the animals, the National Zoo does research in the fields of animal health and behavior and promotes the breeding of endangered species.

112

The Old Stone House, garden side

Naval Observatory, 34th Street and Massachusetts Avenue, NW. The only tours of the observatory are given on Monday—7:30 p.m. (standard time) or 8:30 p.m. (daylight savings time)—to the first 100 persons who show up at the 34th Street gate. The tour lasts about two hours and is not recommended for children under 12. No tours on holidays.

The observatory is the Navy's oldest scientific office dating back to 1830, when it was created out of the office that cared for navigational equipment and prepared charts. The building itself dates from 1893, and its largest telescope is a 26-inch refractor more than 100 years old. Today the observatory provides accurate astronomical time and tracks the movements of the sun, moon, stars, and planets.

Navy Memorial Museum, Washington Navy Yard, 1st and M Streets, SE. Open 9 a.m. to 4 p.m. Monday through Friday and 10 a.m. to 5 p.m. Saturday, Sunday, and holidays. Closed January 1, Thanksgiving, and December 25. Enter 9th Street Gate.

The museum is housed in one of the buildings of a remodeled 19th-century gun factory. The collection documents the history of the U.S. Navy from the days of the Revolutionary War to the present. Currently thousands of naval objects—ship models, weapons, portraits, maps, medals, flags, and special displays—are exhibited in the waterfront museum building and in two outdoor parks. Some exhibits are of the "Do Touch" variety, enabling you to look through periscopes or to aim a gun using the range finder.

Old Stone House, 3051 M Street, NW. Open 9:30 a.m. to 5 p.m. daily. Closed January 1 and December 25.

This is the oldest surviving building in the District of Columbia and is representative of Georgetown in the Revolutionary War period when it was a small, commercial village. Today the Old Stone House has been restored and furnished to reflect those times and the life of working-class people. The flower garden behind the house is an oasis of beauty and calm amidst the bustle and noise of Georgetown.

The Phillips Collection

17 **The Phillips Collection**, 1600 21st Street, NW. Open 10 a.m. to 5 p.m. Tuesday through Saturday and 2 to 7 p.m. Sunday. Closed Mondays, January 1, July 4, Thanksgiving, and December 25. Gift shop. Afternoon concerts are given every Sunday from September through May at 5 p.m.

In 1896 the Phillips family, left the hard winters of Pittsburgh for the milder climate of Washington, D.C. Twenty-five years later Duncan Phillips opened the doors of the family's new home as a public art museum. At the time this was the only museum in the United States dedicated to displaying contemporary art—works of the late-19th and early-20th centuries. Phillips also included paintings by earlier artists whose efforts he perceived as possessing the same innovative qualities. Today the Phillips

Collection contains more than 2,500 pieces of art—most selected by the Phillips family. The same structure, plus additions, contains the collection today. Comfortable chairs in all the rooms make possible the lengthy observation of a favorite picture. While Van Gogh, Monet, Braque, Degas, Rothko, and Picasso are all represented, the acknowledged "star" of the collection is Renoir's "Luncheon of the Boating Party." Most museums in Washington receive tax support, but this is a notable example of private financing and personal art selection.

18 **Rock Creek Park**. The Nature Center is open 9 a.m. to 5 p.m. Tuesday through Sunday. Closed holidays. Pierce Mill is open 9 a.m. to 5 p.m. Wednesday through Sunday. Closed holidays.

From the northern boundary of the city to the National Zoo, Rock Creek Park is a great green wedge aimed at the city's center. It is one of the Nation's earliest large, city parks. This oasis grew out of a search for a new location for the White House shortly after the Civil War. The hope was to find a place in a higher, healthier situation with suitable grounds for a parklike setting. Maj. Nathaniel Michel, the person given the assignment by Secretary of War Edwin Stanton, ended up separating the assignment into two questions and devoting most of his attention to studying possible areas for a park

114

rather than a new location for the White House. He focused on Rock Creek Valley claiming it to be pure fortune that an area of such outstanding beauty was so close to the offices of government. Though a bill establishing a park along the lines Michel proposed passed the Senate it failed in the House. It was not until more than 20 years later that efforts to establish the park met with success. President Benjamin Harrison signed the legislation September 27, 1890— within a few days of establishing Sequoia, Kings Canyon, and Yosemite national parks. From the time of its creation until the National Park Service assumed its administration in 1933, the park was run by the U.S. Army through a Board of Control. In 1917 the Board ordered a report for the future development of the park from the Olmsted Brothers, Inc., whose founder, Frederick Law Olmsted, had been responsible for the development of Central Park in New York City. The plan was finished the next year and became the basis for work in the park. Above all Rock Creek Park is a large chunk of wilderness within the Nation's Capital. In its valley, beneath its canopy of trees live birds, small animals, and wildflowers. The wildflowers begin blooming as early as late February and continue on through the spring and summer. In April thousands of naturalized daffodils grace the slopes of the valley, especially in the lower stretches of the park south of Massachusetts Avenue. In the fall the hardwood trees turn varying shades of red, orange, and gold. Besides being a bit of wilderness in the city the park offers picnic areas, hiking trails, horseback riding, bicycling, tennis courts, an 18-hole golf course, playing fields, the Rock Creek Nature Center, a planetarium, and Pierce Mill. On Saturdays, Sundays, and holidays, Beach Drive between Military and Broad Branch Road is closed to all but bicycles during the daylight hours. This is a part of a bike trail that connects parklands in Maryland with Mount Vernon in Virginia—one of the longest urban bike trails in the United States. From July through Labor Day the Carter Barron Amphitheater offers entertainment. Rock Creek Park provides Washingtonians with almost instant access to an environment that few cities can offer their inhabitants. On these terms it is a treasure and it is perceived as such.

Washington Cathedral

19 **The Textile Museum**, 2320 S Street, NW. Open 10 a.m. to 5 p.m. Tuesday through Saturday and 1 p.m. to 5 p.m. Sunday. Closed national holidays. Museum shop.

The collection consists of some 1,100 outstanding rugs and 14,000 textiles from around the world. It is especially strong in Islamic design, and includes important collections from various regions of Central and South America. Exhibits are changed throughout the year.

20 **The U.S. National Arboretum**, 3501 New York Avenue, NE. Open 8 a.m. to 5 p.m. Monday through Friday and 10 a.m. to 5 p.m. Saturday and Sunday. The National Bonsai Collection is open 10 a.m. to 2:30 p.m. daily. Closed December 25.

This is one of Washington's lesser known treasures.

Azaleas, ferns, camellias, magnolias, rhododendrons, and lilies grow in organized profusion. The Arboretum also has a dwarf conifer collection, hollies, boxwood, and the National Herb Garden. The National Bonsai Collection was a bicentennial gift from Japan. Several trees and shrubs were presented by Soviet Premier Nikita Khrushchev in 1960. The Arboretum also has a specimen of *Franklinia altamaha,* a tree named for Benjamin Franklin and today believed to be extinct in the wild. For anyone interested in trees, shrubs, or woody plants, the Arboretum is a must.

㉑ Washington Cathedral, Massachusetts and Wisconsin Avenues, NW. Open 10 a.m. to 4:30 p.m. daily. The Chapel of the Good Shepherd, which can be entered from the north side, is always open. Services at 8, 9, 10 (from September through June), and 11 a.m. and 4 p.m. on Sunday; 7:30 a.m., noon, and 4 p.m. Monday through Saturday. Tours are given 10 a.m. to 3:15 p.m. Monday through Saturday; 12:15 to 2:45 p.m. Sunday.

This cathedral of the Episcopal Diocese of Washington is modeled on the great Gothic structures of the 14th century and is the sixth largest cathedral in the world. Work began in 1907 and continues on the twin towers. The quality of workmanship —stone and wood carving, stained glass, needlepoint, and metal work—is unsurpassed in this country.

㉒ The Washington Post, 1150 15th Street, NW. Tours are limited to those 11 years and older, 10 a.m. to 3 p.m. on the hour Monday and Thursdays only; reservations required.

One of the most widely circulated and influential newspapers in the country, "The Post" offers a 55-minute tour of its main newsroom, layout and composing floor, and printing presses. Desk-top computers have taken over the job once performed by standard typewriters and linotype machines. The technical aspects of editing by word-processing are emphasized along with information about modern color printing. "The Post" is a morning paper, so the presses don't actually roll until night, but the mood is electric as the news of the day is written, edited, and fitted onto the printed page.

㉓ Woodrow Wilson House, 2340 S Street, NW. Open 10 a.m. to 4 p.m. Tuesday through Sunday. Closed January 1 and December 25. Museum shop. Fee.

When President Woodrow Wilson left the White House on the day of Warren G. Harding's inauguration in 1921, he moved into this brick townhouse and lived here for the remaining three years of his life. Edith Bolling Wilson, who resided here until her death in 1961, bequeathed the property to the National Trust for Historic Preservation.

117

Clara Barton House (left) and
Ft. Washington (below)

Originally all the land that is within District of Columbia was part of Maryland. In colonial times some of Maryland's leading citizens held vast tracts of land in this part of the colony. Georgetown was an important Maryland port. Today Maryland still plays a large role in the affairs of Washington. One of its two suburban counties has more people than the District of Columbia and the other has almost as many. The campus of the National Institutes of Health, Andrews Air Force Base, and the Goddard Space Flight Center assure a substantial federal presence in Montgomery and Prince Georges counties. These locales now are experiencing a transformation that is turning them from bedroom communities into urban centers rivaling the old core of downtown Washington. Lest you should fear that nearby Maryland is turning into faceless steel, concrete, and glass canyons, here are some places to visit that will evoke other days and will show you another side of these vibrant communities. Don't let some of the incongruities fool you, the bedrock of an older Maryland is still there just waiting to be discovered.

24 **Clara Barton National Historic Site**, 5801 Oxford Road, Glen Echo, Maryland. Open 10 a.m. to 5 p.m. daily. Closed January 1, Thanksgiving, and December 25.

When Clara Barton left the scene of the Johnstown, Pennsylvania, flood in 1889, she dismantled one of the Red Cross warehouses of her fledgling organization and took the lumber to Washington, D.C., with her. Two years later she reassembled the structure at Glen Echo, Maryland, intending to use it as a headquarters building for the Red Cross. These plans did not work out immediately, and it was not until 1897 that she used the 38-room structure as an office and a home after making some alterations. Barton lived here until her death in 1912. It became a National Park System site in 1974.

Glen Echo Park, the carousel

Fort Washington, at the end of Fort Washington Road off Indian Head Highway, Maryland. The park is open 7:30 a.m. to dark daily. The fort is open 7:30 a.m. to 5 p.m. September through April; 7:30 a.m. to 8 p.m. May through August. The museum is open daily during the summer and on weekends and holidays the rest of the year. Closed December 25. Fee.

From the early days of Washington's existence, city leaders were concerned with preparing adequate defenses. Several forts have stood on this site; the current one dates from the end of the War of 1812. The fort never saw any action. Yet it remains an outstanding example of early-19th-century military architecture. From the ramparts are panoramic views of the Potomac and of Mount Vernon across the river.

Glen Echo Park, Glen Echo, Maryland. Open 10 a.m. to 5 p.m. Monday through Friday and noon to 5 p.m. Saturday and Sunday.

From May through September a full schedule of folk festivals, concerts, demonstrations, workshops, changing art exhibits, and evening ballroom and square dancing take place. Visit artists' workshops or sign up yourself for classes ranging from ceramics, through dance and music, to painting and drama given in four sessions, year-round. Glen Echo is a community park dedicated to cultural activities similar to those fostering liberal and practical education by the early Chautauquans who established the park in 1891. Buildings with curious names and quaint facades such as Candy Corner, Hall of Mirrors, and Spanish Ballroom recall when Glen Echo was an amusement park and one of the most popular places in Washington. The restored Dentzel Carousel with a Wurlitzer Military 165 band organ still operates and is a joy to see and hear.

Great Falls Tavern, Chesapeake and Ohio Canal National Historical Park, Maryland. The park is open dawn to dusk. Closed December 25. The tavern is open 9 a.m. to 5 p.m. daily. In season, boat rides take visitors through several canal locks.

This historic tavern about 10 miles northwest of Washington was one of the early stopovers on the Chesapeake and Ohio Canal. Today it is preserved by the National Park Service as a museum. The waterway which runs alongside the tavern is one of the best preserved of America's canals.

119

Getting through the Appalachians was a bigger problem than we can begin to appreciate aided as we are by the internal combustion engine and expressways. But for the fast-growing United States of the 1830s the mountains were a formidable barrier. In the late 18th century George Washington had been a stockholder and key figure in the Potowmack Company that sought to construct a canal around the Great Falls of the Potomac in the hope of using the river as a waterway to the interior. Funds were short, however, and little actual work was done. The Erie Canal, opened in 1825, showed that such an ambitious undertaking could be completed. So, on July 4, 1828, President John Quincy Adams turned the first spadeful of earth at the canal's terminus at Georgetown on the Potomac River and work got underway. The same day work began on the Baltimore & Ohio Railroad in Baltimore. By 1850 the canal had made it to Cumberland, Maryland, 184 miles from its beginning, but the railroad had arrived there 8 years earlier. Plans for continuing the canal on to the Ohio River Valley were dropped. Yet the canal functioned until 1924, carrying grain, flour, and coal to tidewater and manufactured goods back to communities between Georgetown and Cumberland. One flood damaged the canal in 1889 and much of it had to be rebuilt. A flood in 1924 coincided with diminishing business and revenues, and the canal was allowed to slip into ruin. The canal was placed under National Park Service administration in 1938, but little interest was shown in it until 1954, when a proposal was made to turn the right-of-way into a four-lane highway. Supreme Court Justice William O. Douglas led the fight to preserve the canal, and it became a national monument in 1961 and a national historical park in 1971. The towpath was dedicated in Douglas's honor in 1974.

28 Greenbelt Park, 6501 Greenbelt Road, Greenbelt, Maryland. Open dawn to dusk daily.

This site tells the story of intensive farming, depletion of minerals, abandonment, extensive erosion, and reclamation. Today this woodland area, managed by the National Park Service, offers overnight camping facilities for visitors to the capital city, hiking trails, and picnic areas.

29 National Aeronautics and Space Administration, Goddard Space Flight Center, Greenbelt, Maryland. Open 10 a.m. to 4 p.m. Wednesday through Sunday. Closed January 1, Thanksgiving, and December 25.

Here NASA keeps track of all the various manmade objects in space and communicates with them. The weather data that we have all become accustomed to seeing on the nightly news is also received here from weather satellites and made available to the domestic media. The tour of the facility shows how this is done and how other information is gleaned from the roving satellites in the sky.

30 National Capital Trolley Museum, on Bonifant Road between Layhill Road and New Hampshire Avenue, Wheaton, Maryland. Open noon to 5 p.m. Saturdays, Sundays, Memorial Day, July 4, and Labor Day and on Wednesday in July and August. Closed December 15 through January 1. Fee for rides.

The museum owns 14 trolleys from the United States and Europe. Some operate through the nearby countryside.

31 Oxon Hill Farm, from Oxon Hill Road off Indian Head Highway, Oxon Hill, Maryland. Open 8:30 a.m. to 5 p.m. daily. Closed December 25.

Small farms like this were common throughout Maryland and Virginia at the turn of the century. A family could largely meet its own needs and grow some crops for market. Most of the work is still done by hand at this National Park System area. Cows are milked by hand, fields are plowed by horse teams, sheep are sheared, and cider is pressed along with other farming activities.

32 Piscataway Park and **National Colonial Farm**, Bryan Point Road, Accokeek, Maryland. The park is open dawn to dusk daily. The farm is open 10 a.m. to 5 p.m. Tuesday through Sunday. Closed January 1, Thanksgiving, and

December 25. Fee.
This restoration of a modest, 18th-century Tidewater plantation sits across the Potomac River from Mount Vernon within Piscataway Park. Costumed farm hands lead tours as they go about raising Red Devon cattle, Chincoteague ponies, turkeys, geese, and Guinea fowl; tending herb and vegetable gardens; and growing crops. The accent is on historical authenticity in this cooperative project between the Accokeek Foundation, Inc., and the National Park Service. Methods not known two centuries ago are not used here. This means that machinery, chemical fertilizers, and pesticides are not used or to be found on the farm. A museum in the Main Barn displays tools that a family living on such a plantation would use for farm work.

Old Town Alexandria (left) and
Arlington House (below)

Crossing any of the bridges over the Potomac leads you to the Old Dominion, the Mother of Presidents, the home of the oldest elected legislature in North America. In other words, you have just entered Virginia. Here settlement by English settlers began. Here much of the agitation that led to the separation from Great Britain got its start. Here the climactic battle of the Revolution was fought and won. Here people attempted to create a separate, sovereign nation from the United States. Much of the history of Virginia mirrors the history of the country, and this is evident in the sites that you can find as you wander throughout the area. Virginia is proud of its past and of its traditions. The people work to preserve that bygone time in the midst of the same rapid urbanization that can be found in the Maryland suburbs. Old Town Alexandria is about the same size as Georgetown with as many 18th and early 19th century homes and buildings. Nearby is Mount Vernon where, across the span of two centuries, you can sense Washington the man. Throughout the region a vibrant, dynamic way of life is supplanting older, slower ways, but many vestiges of the Old Dominion cling on tenaciously.

㉝ **Alexandria**, Virginia. Begin your visit to Alexandria at the Ramsay House Visitors Center, 221 King Street. Open 9 a.m. to 5 p.m. daily. Closed January 1, Thanksgiving, and December 25. This is the visitor center for Alexandria, where you can pick up brochures for shops, restaurants, and hotels, a map with suggested walking tours, and an events calendar. Costumed guides also conduct walking tours, but times vary seasonally.

This was George Washington's hometown. Today many of its streets seem little changed from the way they were 200 years ago, when Alexandria was one of Virginia's largest and most prosperous cities. More than 1,000 18th- and 19th-century homes and structures still stand, a legacy of Alexandria's flourishing past. From its earliest

days the city was a busy river port and tobacco center. The community was founded in July 1749 as Alexandria. Teenager George Washington had assisted surveyor John West, Jr., in laying out the town, and he became intimately involved in many aspects of its life. Sometimes, when it was too late to return to Mount Vernon, he would spend the night at the townhouse he built in 1769; a replica now stands on the site. Traces of the lives of other famous Virginians are found throughout this charming Southern city. The street names themselves reflect the changing allegiances of the citizenry: the earliest ones—King, Queen, Prince—reflecting royalist sentiments while later ones honor patriots of the American Revolution.

34 Arlington House, the Robert E. Lee Memorial, within Arlington National Cemetery. Open daily 9:30 a.m. to 4:30 p.m. October through March; 9:30 a.m. to 6 p.m. April through September.

George Washington Parke Custis began building this house in 1802 and finished it in 1817. The designer was George Hadfield, an English architect. At Custis' death it became the property of his daughter, Mary Custis Lee, the wife of Gen. Robert E. Lee. In those days the estate encompassed the hillside that is now covered with graves. The home, prominently overlooking the Potomac and Washington, D.C., has been restored to its Civil War appearance by the National Park Service and is today a memorial to Lee, a man who gained the respect of Americans both North and South.

35 Arlington National Cemetery, at the west end of Memorial Bridge. Open 8 a.m. to 5 p.m. daily October through March; 8 a.m. to 7 p.m. April through September.

This military burial ground contains the graves of many notable Americans, Presidents John Kennedy and William Howard Taft among them, and the tombs of an unknown soldier from World War I, World War II, the Korean Conflict, and the Vietnam War.

36 Athenaeum, 201 Prince Street, Alexandria, Virginia. Open 10 a.m. to 4 p.m. Tuesday through Saturday and 1 p.m. to 4 p.m. Sunday. Closed holidays and mid-July through Labor Day.

The Northern Virginia Fine Arts Association maintains an art gallery here in an 1850 Greek Revival style building.

Great Falls in late spring

37 Carlyle House, 121 North Fairfax Street, Alexandria, Virginia. Open 10 a.m. to 5 p.m. Tuesday through Saturday and noon to 5 p.m. Sunday. Tours every half hour; last tour at 4:30 p.m. Closed January 1, Thanksgiving, and December 25. Fee; free admission on John Carlyle's birthday, February 7.

This spacious brick home was completed in 1753 by John Carlyle for his bride Sarah Fairfax. In 1755 Maj. Gen. Edward Braddock, commander-in-chief of all British forces in North America, met in this house with five Royal Governors to plan for the campaign against the French and their Indian allies. Tour guides paint a comprehensive picture of mid-18th century life based on a cache of family letters discovered in Scotland. Period furnishings complete the scene.

38 Claude Moore Colonial Farm at Turkey Run, George Washington Memorial Parkway, McLean, Virginia. Open 10 a.m. to 4:30 p.m. Wednesday through Sunday, April through December. Fee.

A working tenant farm on a few hilly acres just a few minutes from the busy parkway takes visitors back to Colonial times. Programs are announced during the planting and harvesting seasons. There is always something for children to learn and to do.

39 Friendship Fire Engine Company, 107 South Alfred Street, Alexandria, Virginia. Open irregularly; check with the Ramsay House Visitors Center.

A volunteer fire company was organized here in 1774, and its first fire engine came from a member, George Washington.

40 George Washington Memorial Parkway, Virginia and Maryland.

The parkway was carefully engineered in the 1930s to enhance views from the tidewater lowlands to high palisades further upstream, and to link together a variety of historic sites and recreation areas along the way. Notable are parking and picnicking overlooks at Fort Hunt and Fort Marcy, sailing marinas at Belle Haven and Daingerfield Island, a 17-mile-long pedestrian/bike path, and nature trails such as the one through the Dyke Marsh wildlife preserve. It provides a direct link between several sites associated with George Washington: Washington, D.C., whose site he chose; Alexandria, where he conducted his business; and Mount Vernon, where he made his home.

The Masonic Memorial

41 George Washington Masonic National Memorial, King and Callahan Streets, Alexandria, Virginia. Open 9 a.m. to 5 p.m. daily. Closed January 1, Thanksgiving, and December 25.

When the Alexandria Masonic Lodge was organized in 1788, George Washington was its first worshipful master. Today masons honor him with this memorial, which contains Washington memorabilia. Murals and stained glass windows depict events of Washington's life. You can take an elevator to an observation area for a view of Alexandria and beyond to Washington. It is, indeed, one of the finest vantage points in the entire metropolitan area—especially on a clear day.

42 Great Falls Park, intersection of Old Dominion Drive and Old Georgetown Pike, Great Falls, Virginia. Open 9 a.m. to dark daily. Closed December 25. Fee.

Here the Potomac River cascades over a jagged rock wall and races through a narrow gorge in its headlong rush to reach tidewater, just a few miles away. Hiking and horseback riding trails wander through the woods and along the gorge. At times of flooding, the narrow gorge constricts the river, backing it up and almost obliterating the falls. In the hopes of fostering waterborne transportation and trade with the West, George Washington promoted the idea of building the Potowmack Canal around the falls. The project was never fully realized, but the remains of the canal and some locks can be seen today in this National Park System site.

127

Gunston Hall

The Lyceum

An exhibit at the Lyceum

43 Gunston Hall Plantation, Lorton, Virginia. Open 9:30 a.m. to 5 p.m. daily. Closed December 25. Fee.

Below Mount Vernon on the Potomac River, this beautiful 550-acre estate was the home of George Mason, who was the author of the Fairfax Resolves and the Virginia Declaration of Rights. The latter became the basis of the Bill of Rights, the first 10 amendments to the U.S. Constitution. Mason, a major framer of the Constitution, refused to sign the document because it lacked the safeguards later incorporated into the Bill of Rights and because it failed to abolish the slave trade. Many architectural historians consider the interior of Mason's brick mansion to be among the finest in the United States. The elaborate woodwork and detailing are representative of the work being done in London during the mid-18th century. The designer was William Buckland and the woodworker was William Sears. Reconstruction of the formal gardens surrounding the 18th-century boxwood allée was an early project of the Garden Club of Virginia.

44 Lee-Fendall House, 614 Oronoco Street, Alexandria, Virginia. Open 10 a.m. to 4 p.m. Tuesday through Saturday; noon to 4 p.m. Sunday. Closed January 1, Thanksgiving, and December 25. Fee.

Phillip Richard Fendall built this house in 1789. Fendall was related to the Lee family; in 118 years, 39 different Lees lived in this house. Here "Light Horse Harry" wrote the funeral oration that described Washington as "first in war, first in peace, and first in the hearts of his countrymen." The last private owner of the house was labor leader John L. Lewis, who died in 1969.

45 The Lyceum, 201 South Washington Street, Alexandria, Virginia. Open 10 a.m. to 5 p.m. daily. Closed January 1, Thanksgiving, and December 25. The gift shop specializes in items from Alexandria and Virginia.

Located in an imposing Greek revival building, which has also been used as the Alexandria Library Company, a Civil War hospital, and a private home, The Lyceum interprets life in Northern Virginia during the past 300 years. Changing exhibits, as well as concerts, lectures, and films, provide a vivid picture of the area and of the times.

128

LBJ Grove

Manassas National Battlefield Park, summertime twilight

46 Lyndon Baines Johnson Memorial Grove on the Potomac, in **Lady Bird Johnson Park** on Columbia Island in the Potomac River, accessible from the George Washington Memorial Parkway.

In honor of the 36th President, who said his "deepest attitudes and beliefs were shaped by a closeness with the land," a 43-ton, rough-hewn block of granite quarried in Johnson's native Texas stands in a grove of white pines and dogwoods. The memorial is reached by several footpaths bordered by azaleas, rhododendrons, and the seasonal flowering of thousands of daffodils. The park is named for the former First Lady whose concern for the environment sparked beautification efforts nationwide. Every spring the shores of the Potomac pay tribute to her vision.

47 Manassas National Battlefield Park, Manassas, Virginia. Open daily. Closed December 25. Fee.

Northerners came to know the battles here as first and second Bull Run, while Southerners called them first and second Manassas. Whatever the name, both were Southern victories. The first battle meant that the war would not be a short one, and the second opened the way for a Southern invasion of the North that led to the Battle of Antietam. Today the National Park Service provides a walking tour of the First Battle of Manassas and a driving tour of the Second Battle. Exhibits in the visitor center explain the events that led to the battles, what went on during the fighting, and what happened afterward.

48 Mount Vernon. Southern terminus of the George Washington Memorial Parkway. Mount Vernon is open every day of the year: 9 a.m. to 4 p.m. November to March; 9 a.m. to 5 p.m. March to November. Fee.

For more than half his life Mount Vernon belonged to George Washington. No matter where events took him, this was the place to which he returned. Under Washington's direction, Mount Vernon became one of Virginia's outstanding plantations. Today the mansion has been restored to look as nearly as possible as it did during Washington's lifetime. The tombs of George and Martha Washington and some other family members are also located on the grounds. Some of the trees near the house were planted by Washington.

129

The Mount Vernon we see today is due to the work of two people who never knew one another – George Washington and Ann Pamela Cunningham. The first developed it, the second preserved it. Mount Vernon had been family property almost a century when George Washington inherited it in 1761. Until his death Washington lavished time – as much as he could spare – and love on his home. Washington always maintained his interest in his estate, followed all developments closely no matter how far

away he was or for how long he had been absent, and thought himself a fortunate man to have such an excellent property. "No estate in United America is more pleasantly situated than this," he wrote to one correspondent. Under his watchful eye, Mount Vernon increased from 2,126 acres to more than 8,000 on five independently managed farms. Washington never bought or sold any slaves after the Revolution and owned only those he inherited, that Martha brought to their marriage, and their de-

scendants. On his death he freed his personal servant, and his will provided that all the remaining slaves be freed on his wife's death. Service buildings and workshops were built over the years, and gardens and fields laid out all according to Washington's strict instruction. He liked to think of himself as an innovative and skillful farmer, and he experimented with different crops. Washington died in the last days of 1799 and his wife, Martha, survived him not quite three years. Thereafter the property passed to other

family members who found the task of running the plantation increasingly onerous. Different family members tried to persuade either the Federal Government or the Commonwealth of Virginia to maintain the land in trust for the people of the United States. Neither argument was successful. In 1853 Ann Pamela Cunningham of South Carolina created the Mount Vernon Ladies' Association of the Union, which drummed up interest in preserving the home. In 1858 the mansion, major outbuildings, and 200 acres of Washington's land became the property of the Association. Since that time the Association has engaged in research, preservation, routine maintenance, and any work needed to keep Mount Vernon open to the public.

49 The Pentagon, intersection of I-395 and Va. 110, Arlington, Virginia. Tours 9:30 a.m. to 3:30 p.m. Monday through Friday except 10:30 a.m. and 1 and 3 p.m. Closed weekends and holidays.

This is the home of the Department of Defense. It is the largest office building in the world.

50 Prince William Forest Park, Triangle, Virginia. Open daily. Fee.

The land here was acquired and reclaimed by the Civilian Conservation Corps as a demonstration project in the 1930s. Today a pine and hardwood forest shades a National Park System area that is laced with hiking trails; has campgrounds for campers, groups, and trailers; and provides walks, talks, and exhibits.

51 The Boyhood Home of Robert E. Lee, 607 Oronoco Street, Alexandria, Virginia. Open 10 a.m. to 4 p.m. Monday through Saturday; noon to 4 p.m. Sunday. Closed December 15 through February 1. Fee.

Henry "Light Horse Harry" Lee and his wife—Ann Hill Carter Lee—moved into this house with their five children, including 5-year-old Robert E. Lee. The house, which was built in 1795, has been restored and furnished with rare antiques, and memorabilia of the Lee family.

52 Stabler Leadbeater Apothecary Shop, 105 South Fairfax Street, Alexandria, Virginia. Open 10 a.m. to 4:30 p.m. Monday through Saturday. Because of major renovations, check with Ramsay House Visitors Center for times.

This shop first opened for business in 1792 and operated until 1933. Today it is a museum that houses a remarkable collection of early medical wares. Robert E. Lee was in this store when Lt. J.E.B. Stuart delivered a message telling Lee to go to Harpers Ferry to deal with John Brown's raid in 1859.

53 Theodore Roosevelt Island, in the Potomac River, accessible from the northbound lanes of the George Washington Memorial Parkway on a footbridge at the parking lot. Open 8 a.m. to dark daily.

This island commemorates Theodore Roosevelt's love of nature and his enduring commitment to conservation. Four granite tablets, near a statue of Roosevelt, contain selections from his writings. Trails lead through woods and swamps in this refuge from the nearby city.

U.S. Marine Corps War Memorial, dawn

Theodore Roosevelt Island

54 **U.S. Marine Corps War Memorial** and the **Netherlands Carillon**, Virginia. Marine sunset review parade June through August 7 p.m. to 8:30 p.m. Tuesdays. Carillon concerts April through June and September 2 to 4 p.m. on Saturdays; during July and August 6:30 to 8:30 p.m. on Saturdays.

The popular sculpture by Felix W. de Weldon, based on a prize news photo by Joe Rosenthal, captures the agony of World War II in a tribute to all the Marine Corps engagements since 1775. Suspended nearby in an open tower is a 49-bell carillon dedicated to friendship from the Dutch people for American aid received during and after World War II.

The gristmill's works

Wolf Trap Farm Park, the Filene Center

55 Washington's Grist Mill Historical State Park, Mount Vernon, Virginia. Open daily Memorial Day to Labor Day, February 22, and on the commemoration of Washington's birthday.

In 1770 George Washington constructed a mill on or near this site to replace one that had fallen into disrepair. Washington's mill ground two different grades of flour: "merchant trade" and "country trade." Washington operated the mill throughout his life and left it to his nephew, Lawrence Lewis, the owner of nearby Woodlawn. By 1850 the mill had fallen into ruins and many of the stones had been used for other buildings. In 1932, the bicentennial of Washington's birth, the Commonwealth of Virginia reconstructed the mill.

56 Wolf Trap Farm Park for the Performing Arts, 1551 Trap Road, Vienna, Virginia. Open early June through early September. Other programs, smaller in scope, go on year round. Pre-performance picnics on the lawns are encouraged.

Situated only 25 minutes west of the White House, Wolf Trap was the first National Park System unit dedicated to the performing arts. Programs in the Filene Center are designed to suit a variety of interests. The best in opera, dance, symphony, jazz, musical theater, and popular music is presented here. The Wolf Trap Company provides young artists with an opportunity to work with professionals. The theater seats 3,500 people under cover and 3,000 more on the lawn.

57 Woodlawn Plantation and **Frank Lloyd Wright's Pope-Leighey House**, Mount Vernon, Virginia. Woodlawn is open 9:30 a.m. to 4:30 p.m. daily. Closed January 1, Thanksgiving, and December 25. Check with the staff for information on seeing the Pope-Leighey House. Fee.

When Washington's foster daughter, Eleanor Parke Custis, married his nephew, Maj. Lawrence Lewis, Washington gave them a large tract of his Mount Vernon estate on which to build a home and here they built Woodlawn. The architect is believed to have been Dr. William Thornton, who designed the Capitol. The Pope-Leighey House, also on the property, is a Frank Lloyd Wright Usonian house, built in 1940. Both structures are the property of the National Trust for Historic Preservation.

134

Woodlawn Plantation

Pope—Leighey House

Part 3

Washington Sampler and Adviser

Join the Celebration

"The population of Washington is more like that of Paris or Vienna than of the usual American city," journalist Frank Carpenter wrote near the end of the last century. "The people are more interested in amusement than in work, and a celebration of any kind is sure of a large attendance."

Alas, in the years since, the work has grown more serious in Washington—and the workers more serious with it—but the city's love of celebration survives unchecked.

Like few other capitals in the world, Washington was laid out for ceremony, appropriately by a Parisian borrowing heavily from his native city. Some of Pierre Charles L'Enfant's plan never saw the light of day: Constitution Avenue, for example, is no longer a canal. Still, L'Enfant imposed a logic of gaiety and grandeur that has been with Washington ever since.

Nowhere is that more obvious than in the wonderfully conceived triangle joining the Capitol, White House, and Washington Monument, the nearest thing this country has to a national party park. In June and early July, the Smithsonian museums that dot the Mall and the National Park Service play host to the American Folklife Festival. On July 4th the Nation's birthday is celebrated with a spectacular fireworks display that attracts hundreds of thousands of spectators.

That same month, on the Ellipse south of the White House, the twilight military tatoos begin. On the same site in December, the President turns on the lights of the National Christmas Tree, and weeks of nightly choral performances begin. A few weeks later, the restored Post Office Building on Pennsylvania Avenue becomes the setting for a giddy New Year's Eve Party.

In spring, the ornamental cherry trees bloom along the Tidal Basin south of the Mall, and another festival begins. Remarkably, the trees almost always bloom right on cue.

These are Washington's parties—that's the fun of living here—but they also are the Nation's parties because Washington is the Nation's city.

The city, however, does enjoy an occasional provincial celebration. Some times, on Sunday evenings in the fall and early winter, tourists are startled by impromptu parades of motorists honking horns and raising "V" for victory signs out their car windows. A diplomatic or military triumph? No, it's just another professional football victory for the locally beloved Washington Redskins.

Pages 136-137: "The President's Own" United States Marine Band

138

L'Enfant's great radial avenues are host to another enduring part of Washington's ceremonial life: the motorcade. Security precautions have made the business of transporting heads of state more icily remote than in the days when Abraham Lincoln and Walt Whitman could nod a greeting to each other. Today, you need penetrating vision to see the grand personage in the center limousine behind thick, tinted glass. But even the natives stop and stare, sometimes from the attendant traffic jams.

It's important to note that ceremony works its way into the whole fabric of life in Washington. The sombre, stately changing of the guard at Arlington Cemetery's Tomb of the Unknown Soldier, the ritualized greeting of foreign dignitaries at the White House, the parades and balls that mark the quadrennial inaugural ceremonies, the frequent wreath layings—at the Lincoln Memorial on Abraham Lincoln's birthday, at the Washington Monument on George Washington's birthday—they all date back to an elegant plan that built ceremony into the very soul of the place.

—*Howard Means*, **Washington-based newspaper columnist and writer**

Think Thematically

When many people come to Washington they have a long list of specific sites they want to see, and they head right out to see them. After trudging around the city all day, they return to their motel or hotel with weary feet and dizzy heads.

There's no need to do that. Relax a bit while you are here. Have a picnic on the Mall or along the Potomac. Take a bike ride on the trail that runs along the George Washington Memorial Parkway north of Mount Vernon. Go to an armed services band concert or to a show at one of the area's many professional and amateur theaters. Take a leisurely walk through or by the city's innumerable floral gardens. Savor the District's international ambience at one of the many new ethnic restaurants.

Instead of looking at the city as an endless string of individual sites, think of it thematically. Consider making up your own day-long tour of the city's statues and fountains, or taking an architecturally oriented tour in the blocks around the White House. You might be surprised—and delighted—by what you discover when the statuary becomes more than a backdrop and when the buildings become more than depositories of historic objects.

Some times the not-so-well-known places are the ones that you remember best when you regale your friends and neighbors with tales about your trip. There are all sorts of small, delightful museums and historic sites for you to discover and enjoy. The extra effort to ferret out these places is usually well

U.S. Navy Band on the Mall

worth it. Be adventurous. Let serendipity be your guide.

And if you have children in tow on your pilgrimage to the Nation's Capital, keep their interests—and attention spans—in mind. As an additional challenge, they might follow Henry Fairlie's advice in Part 1 and read the inscriptions on the government buildings.

To help you plan your Washington visit, the following pages present a thematic sampler of the metropolitan area along with suggestions for side trips you might take to National Park System sites and other places in the neighboring states of Virginia, Maryland, West Virginia, and Pennsylvania. Enjoy your travels.

—*The National Park Service*

Floral Vistas

While in Washington, take a moment to stop and smell the roses . . . and the daffodils and the tulips and the cherry blossoms and the azaleas and the dogwood and . . . . In almost any month, somewhere in the city, there is a blooming spectacle of flowers guaranteed to elicit a chorus of "oohs" and "ahs."

The most celebrated of the city's floral displays are the delicate white and pink blossoms of the Japanese cherry trees that decorate the Tidal Basin, the Washington Monument grounds, and adjacent downtown parks in spring. But spring is also the season of daffodils, tulips, and other early bloomers. Daffodils put on some of their gaudiest shows around the Tidal Basin, in nearby Lady Bird Johnson Park, and in the woodland setting of Rock Creek Park, where more than a million explode in sunbursts of yellow. Well over 100,000 tulips planted by the National Park Service each year enliven Washington's avenues, urban parks, squares, monuments,

and fountains. One particularly ambitious display is the Tulip Library (shown here) beside the Tidal Basin, where as many as 90 varieties bloom red, white, blue, yellow, purple, and just about any other color imaginable. A more traditional combination of red and yellow tulips brightens the White House lawn; up-close peeks at the First Family's gardens, including the famed Rose Garden, are provided on tours on two days each April. Other gardens at Rawlins Park, Old Stone House, Pershing Park, and

Above: Smithsonian's Enid A. Haupt Garden
Background: Tulip Library near Tidal Basin

Meridian Hill Park are some of the city's best kept and most enchanting secrets.

Spring's flowers fade quickly, but gardeners replace them with begonias, marigolds, impatiens, and other summer annuals that bloom into fall. By late-spring, or early-summer, it is the season of azaleas, when all of Washington seems to be ablaze in brilliant pinks, reds, and lavenders. Nowhere are the azaleas more dazzling than at the National Arboretum, where 70,000 of them burst into bloom among dogwoods, magnolias, and other flowering shrubs and trees. Another place where flowers bloom almost all year is the U.S. Botanic Garden, which boasts a collection of exotic orchids, as well as other unusual tropical and desert plants. Flowers of quite a different type highlight Kenilworth Aquatic Gardens, where summer-blooming water lilies and lotuses abound.

And how do the gardens of the rich and famous grow? Quite nicely, as demonstrated by the formal European-style gardens of Dumbarton Oaks. Intermixed with fountains, pools, and sculpted hedges are terraces of roses, forsythias, and cherry trees. Another formal delight is the Smithsonian's Enid A. Haupt Garden (inset).

For those who prefer flowers wild, there are forested trails through Rock Creek Park and the Chesapeake and Ohio Canal National Historical Park.

— *Carolyn de Raismes*, **NPS writer-editor**

The statues and fountains of Washington document the District's role not just as a center of the Federal Government but as a repository for monuments to all aspects of the collective national memory.

The city's parks are full of artifacts made by one generation to celebrate its own and earlier times and to make sure that later generations will remember. These artifacts, cast in bronze or carved in stone, are permanent emblems of professional, social, or tribal identities; of deeds performed; of fears averted; of victories; and of survivals that some people could not bear to have their children forget.

The events and heroes commemorated have roots in every state of the Union. While the more important monuments were approved by Congress, few were built with appropriated funds.

The public subscription for the Washington Monument stretched out over several decades. On the other hand it took little more than a year to commit $7 million for the capital's most visited and most intensely revered monument, the Vietnam Veterans Memorial. The funds were raised by the Vietnam veterans themselves.

Some of the city's statues are frankly polemic: Temperance. Some are chauvinistic: Shevchenko. Some are fraternal: Arlington Jaycees. Some are controversial: Dr. Samuel Hahnemann, the homeopathy advocate. Some are poignant: Gallaudet, the creator of sign language for the deaf. Some are brooding: Augustus Saint-Gaudens' Adams Monument, also known as Grief (below left). Some are plain bathetic like the Boy Scout Memorial, a boy with a knotted neck scarf flanked by two unclad parents. "If granite could blush," one critic remarked, "the scout would turn crimson."

Perhaps the city's most unofficial-looking piece of outdoor sculpture was commissioned by the American Medi-

From left: Grief, Bartholdi Fountain, Navy-Marine Memorial

cal Association. It is the abstract stabile Sky Landscape, the only public work in the capital by Louise Nevelson, the grand dame of American sculpture.

There appears to be emerging a trend for sculpture designed to be "read" by motorists. Examples are J. Seward Johnson, Jr.'s The Awakening, an aluminum giant whose right knee, right arm, left hand, and bearded face are trying to squirm their way out of the earth at the tip of Hains Point; and the lyrical Navy-Marine Memorial with its seven gulls hovering over a breaking wave of art nouveau aluminum (below) along George Washington Memorial Parkway opposite the Pentagon.

Continued on next page

Water, Bronze, and Stone

Some motorists—and ambitious pedestrians—come across the largest and most successful of the city's numerous statues to generals, the Grant Memorial at the east end of the Mall. Though overshadowed by the Capitol, the 252-foot-long statuary grouping is a masterpiece in itself. Ulysses S. Grant sits serenely on horseback flanked by highly charged battle scenes of artillery and cavalry (below).

Some of the newest memorials are low and flat, best seen from a helicopter: Memorial to 56 Signers of the Declaration of Independence in Constitution Gardens, and Freedom Plaza, a giant flat map of Washington with patriotic quotations at Pennsylvania Avenue at 14th Street, NW.

All these inert masses are relieved by the daily changing sunlight and shadows, by seasonal bloomings, or sometimes by splashing water. The parks and avenues abound in fountains, many of them virtuoso compositions of sprays

of water playing over polished metal and granite. The cast-iron Bartholdi Fountain (page 144), by the Statue of Liberty sculptor, was the city's first to incorporate sound and light.

How many people realize when they see the letters "D.C." on a license plate who the place was named for? The rationale is fully documented in the forecourt of Union Station with the Christopher Columbus Memorial Fountain, where children sneak forbidden dips all summer in the shadow of Columbus' ship.

At the steps of the Library of Congress sculptor Roland Hinton Perry carved an ornate Fountain of the Court of Neptune, a colossal old man of the sea with tritons and mermaids in a frenzy of harnessed energy. At the Washington Hebrew Congregation, a fountain rises from an abstract seven-branched menorah of stainless steel in the form of the Hebrew letter Yod, which symbolizes the name of God. Not

Above right: Meridian Hill Park
Background: Grant Memorial

far away, in the Garth Fountain at Washington Cathedral, is an abstract lotus by George Tsutakawa. Pumps hidden within its stacked leafy forms make for a lively integration of falling water and shining bronze. A cascade of 13 graduated, curved fountains ending in a pool and promenade accentuates the delightful formal garden aspect of Meridian Hill Park (left) on 16th Street NW.

And perhaps the city's most urbane fountain is Malabar by Elyn Zimmerman at the National Geographic: five spit-and-polished reddish boulders flanking a long reflecting pool.

Excluding the Zero Milestone, only two monuments relate exclusively to the District of Columbia itself: the D.C. World War Memorial and the District Settlers. This tells you something about the capital: it belongs to the Nation.

— *E.J. Applewhite*, **essayist and author**

The Performing Arts

There's no business like show business, and there's an awful lot of it in Washington.

The center for the performing arts is, conveniently, the John F. Kennedy Center for the Performing Arts. In four theaters—sometimes five—under that roof, you can see ballet and opera from Washington and elsewhere, foreign and domestic, the National Symphony and visiting orchestras, a wide variety of concert artists, musicals, and straight dramas and comedies pre-Broadway, post-Broadway, and originating at the Ken Cen. You want it, they've got it—at one time or another.

The other Broadway-conscious house in town is the city's oldest continuously operating, The National Theater, which is now featuring almost exclusively pre-New York tryouts and national touring companies of New York hits.

The city's home-grown leader of the country's regional theater movement is Arena Stage, which uses both the in-the-round house for which the theater is named and a lovely small proscenium arch house, the Kreeger, as well as a subterranean cabaret, The Old Vat, where experimental works-in-progress often appear. Arena's scenic effects are often dazzling, the acting on a high level, the choice of plays always interesting, often inspired.

The other institutional house in town is the Folger Theater on Capitol Hill, where a replica of Shakespeare's Globe Theater is used for Shakespearean productions and much else besides.

Ford's Theatre, downtown, was closed after Abraham Lincoln's assassination, but in recent years it has been brought back to its show business purposes. It specializes in one-man shows based on the letters and journals of literary and historical figures and also presents tabloid musicals and small-cast plays.

The hottest of the younger companies in town for the last several years has been the Studio Theatre, with one

From left: National Symphony Orchestra, Folger Shakespeare Library production, Royal Danish Ballet

knockout production after another. The New Playwrights is just what it says, with the pluses and minuses of the name.

Far-out theater—outside the city that is—is good, too. Wolf Trap, to the west in Virginia, is enjoyable for summertime musicals, concerts, and specials, combined with a picnic on the grass. To the north, and very good indeed, is Olney, Maryland's State Summer Theater.

Concerts take place at the Library of Congress, the Phillips Collection, the Corcoran Gallery, and especially at the National Gallery of Art, which maintains its own chamber orchestra. Church and State alike offer first-class free musical programs: check the Washington Cathedral, the Shrine of the Immaculate Conception, and the National Presbyterian Church; the Armed Services bands—all of them—keep on the move around town, but they're well worth finding and offer a lot more than oom-pa-pa, although their oom-pa-pa is the best. For other musical tastes, there are a few jazz and bluegrass clubs around Washington.

And the great thing about them all is that, after a hard day of museums and monuments, you take in the performing arts sitting down.

—*Frank Getlein*, **Washington theater, movie, and restaurant critic**

Small and Multifarious Museums

Washington's museums, like American culture, are a healthy blend of pomp and pop, of the conventional and the eccentric. On the Mall, the familiar, dignified repositories of the Nation's heritage stand at attention. But elsewhere in the city are some well-kept secrets.

Some of these museums remind us that we are a nation of nations. The B'nai B'rith Klutznick Museum wraps history, archeology, art, and religion into an intriguing package appealing to both the eye and the mind. The permanent collection highlights Jewish life and festivals with ceremonial, utilitarian, and art objects from 20 centuries. And the Lillian and Albert Small Jewish Museum tells the story of Washington's Jewish community.

Howard University, on the edge of the historic black residential area of LeDroit Park, has a world-renowned collection that preserves black history and cultural heritage. The materials in the Moorland-Spingarn Research Center

come to life through permanent and temporary exhibitions at the Howard University Museum. Across the Quadrangle, Howard's Gallery of Art has changing exhibitions and its own African art collection (below center).

Other museums offer a combination of ambience and history. The manicured summer flower beds that ornament Anderson House, the headquarters of the Society of the Cincinnati, are reason enough for a visit beyond the exhibits of Revolutionary War memorabilia.

Although the city's approach to the visual arts can be considered staid, the Washington Project for the Arts is a leading showcase for contemporary art in a variety of media. Nearby, in WPA's 7th Street neighborhood, are a number of contemporary arts and crafts galler-

From left: National Museum of Women in the Arts, Howard University Gallery of Art, National Building Museum

ies. And if you like rugs, blankets, and other things woven or knitted, go to the Textile Museum. Another esthetic delight is Dumbarton Oaks, which is devoted to an unusual combination of Byzantine and pre-Columbian arts.

A lesser-known site is the Building Museum (below right), and you should see it for the building itself, if nothing else. Eight huge Corinthian columns dominate this, the largest room in the city. Other lesser-knowns include such specialized governmental collections as the Armed Forces Medical Museum, the Navy Museum, and the U.S. Department of the Interior Museum—all of which are well worth seeing. And Washington's array of museums keeps expanding. More than 190 women artists from the Re-

naissance to the present are represented at the National Museum of Women in the Arts. If you haven't heard of Lavinia Fontana, you're not alone, but this new museum celebrates the work of women like Fontana—a respected artist in Bologna in the 1500s—as well as the better known Mary Cassatt, Georgia O'Keeffe, and Helen Frankenthaler. A 1907 Masonic temple designed by Waddy Wood houses the museum (below left).

The National Holocaust Memorial Museum, opening in the early 1990s, commemorates the six million Jews murdered during the Holocaust and the millions of other victims of Nazism.

With Washington's bounty of cultural attractions, the easy decision is to head for the Mall. Occasionally the more pleasurable option is to visit some of the city's other treasures.

—*Ellen Cochran Hirzy*, **freelance writer-editor and former editor of "Museum News"**

Some parts of the Nation's Capital are more enjoyable than others—at least from a child's perspective. Parents usually want their children to see the White House, the Capitol, and the Smithsonian museums before heading home, but some not-quite-so-obvious places and events might impress them as much.

Take the kids to the Capital Children's Museum, where they can stretch their minds with computers and innovative exhibits, pretend they are firefighters, and otherwise have a good time. The secret of this place is activity, and the kids welcome it after hours of trooping around museums looking at artifacts.

Whether or not you have a zoo in your hometown, spend a morning or afternoon at the National Zoo. The Smithsonian has gone to great pains to make the animals' habitats more natural and less cage-like. The panda bears are perhaps the major attraction— except to the boy or girl who prefers giraffes or elephants or gorillas.

If your children know little about rural farm life, take a short drive into nearby Maryland to Oxon Hill Farm or to the National Colonial Farm to see some farm animals up close. Oxon Hill takes you back to the early 1900s, and Colonial portrays a mid-18th century middle-class tobacco farm. In McLean, Virginia, the Claude Moore Colonial Farm provides a glimpse of life on a modest family homestead.

You can take a ride into other days-gone-by at the National Capital Trolley Museum and at the Chesapeake and Ohio Canal. At the museum, not only will you see streetcars from grandma and grandpa's day, but you can take a 20-minute trolley ride. In every season but winter you can ride mule-drawn canal boats in restored sections of the C&O Canal at Georgetown and at Great Falls, Maryland, while interpreters tell canal stories and sing songs.

Or you can take a trip back to the Victorian era at the Washington Dolls' House and Toy Museum in Chevy Chase, D.C., which is full of—what else? —dollhouses, dolls, and toys.

If your kids want a diversion while you're on the Mall, let them crawl over the dinosaur and ride the carousel. Then take them to the Insect Zoo in the Museum of Natural History to see, among other things, bees and tarantulas. They might even get to hold a Madagascar hissing cockroach.

And, when you are worn out but the kids are still full of energy, suggest they throw a frisbee or fly a kite on the Washington Monument grounds, or let them work their legs on a Tidal Basin paddleboat. While they unwind, you can, too, and soon you will be ready for another round of sightseeing in the mandatory marble corridors.

— Bruce Hopkins,
NPS writer-editor

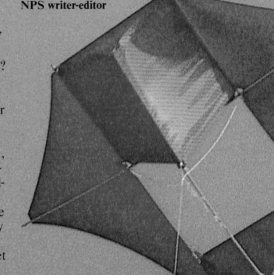

From left: Young firefighter at Capital Children's Museum, clown, watching a patriotic parade

International Washington

In the last 30 years or so, Washington has changed from a sleepy Southern town to a bustling, growing, cosmopolitan city of fashionable shops and sidewalk cafes—a Paris on the Potomac.

International artists perform in the city's concert halls and theaters; the museums, in addition to their rich permanent collections, exhibit works from all over the world in traveling shows attracting thousands of visitors; the Smithsonian Institution has expanded its collection with the spectacular underground Sackler Gallery of Near Eastern and Asian Art and the Museum of African Art; and the intellectual life of the universities is flourishing.

The most casual observer can't miss one sign of this surge in internationalism: the growth of the restaurant community in which more than 50 nationalities are now represented. An earlier handful of bland French, Italian, and Chinese restaurants has been replaced by an astonishing variety of regional eateries from Provence, Northern Italy, and Szechuan Province that rival the best of their own countries. Other restaurants reflect every taste and cuisine of the world. One can dine on food from countries as far flung as Afghanistan, Vietnam, Ethiopia, Korea, El Salvador, and Thailand—with several serving the fiery food of the latter.

The clientele for these restaurants is drawn from many sources: locals, diplomats, tourists, and expatriates. International organizations such as the World Bank, the International Monetary Fund, and the Organization of American

States bring large numbers of employees and their families from all over the world.

The diplomatic community with all its comings and goings also makes up a significant part of the international community here. Massachusetts Avenue NW., between Dupont Circle and Wisconsin Avenue, passes as "embassy row" with clusters of embassies housed in their own elegant buildings like the British and Brazilian, or in grand old 19th-centry mansions converted to serve the 20th like the Indonesian and Turkish missions. The blue-and-white tiled Islamic Center with its mosque and exotic minarets is just down the street from the former Iranian mission and the South African embassy, both of which have been centers of attention

as world events continue to put their mark on the city. You will find other embassies located in various parts of the city, such as the modern structures housing French diplomats, near Georgetown University (below), and our Canadian neighbors, across from the National Gallery.

Children from embassy families often attend one of several international schools scattered around the city, but some countries run their own.

One of the most obvious signs of diplomatic presence can be spotted by any passer-by: the red, white, and blue registration plates on some cars marked with a D and a secret code (for security reasons) identifying the country and diplomatic status of the owner.

Continued on next page

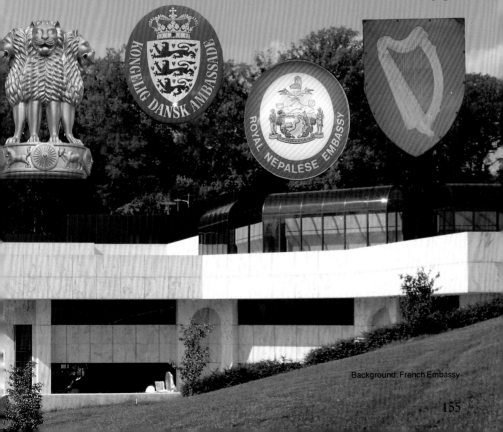

Background: French Embassy

International Washington

Although Washington, D.C., in the past has never been a haven for large numbers of immigrants, in the past decade the city has found itself the beneficiary of an influx of Hispanics from Central America and the Caribbean, of Vietnamese and other Southeast Asians, and to a lesser degree of refugees from the Middle East. These new residents have brought with them the customs, languages, and food of their homelands.

Thousands, for instance, take to the streets to celebrate Hispanic culture every July in the Adams-Morgan street

Above: Ethnic festival musicians
Background: Chinese New Year dragon

festival with food, song, and dance. Every Chinese New Year, an exotic dragon (below) winds its way in a parade through Washington's Chinatown with the sound of firecrackers chasing away the evil spirits. The streets of Clarendon in the Virginia suburbs are lined with shops selling Vietnamese fermented fish sauce, taro leaves, and Oriental melons. Even the supermarket chains have opened stores to cater to the international population, offering delicacies ranging from English chocolate biscuits and Russian caviar to Mexican peppers and Chinese mushrooms.

America and Americans have made citizens of the world, as well as the citizens of the 50 states, welcome in their elegant and intriguing capital. This international flavor has added color, culture, and sophistication to the District of Columbia's tradition of history, politics, and patriotism.

–Brigitte Weeks, **editor-in-chief, Book-of-the-Month Club**

Regional Side Trips

PENNSYLVANIA

Harrisburg
State capital

Hopewell
Furnace NHS

PHILADEL
Independence N
18th century bui
Museums, sports

Ephrata Cloister
Landis Valley
Farm Museum

**PENNSYLVANIA
DUTCH COUNTRY**

Valley
Forge NHP

York
Manufacturing center
Agricultural products

Lancaster
18th & 19th century buildings
Agricultural products

Longwood Gardens

Brandywine
Battlefield SP

Hagerstown
Manufacturing center
Agricultural products

Catoctin
Mountain Park

Gettysburg
Gettysburg NMP
Eisenhower NHS

WILMINGTON
Chemical products
Winterthur Museum

MARYLAND

Cunningham Falls SP

**WEST
VIRGINIA**

Antietam
NB

Frederick
18th and 19th century buildings
Dairy products

Hampton NHS

New Castle
18th century
buildings

**NEW
JERSE**

Harpers
Ferry NHP

BALTIMORE
Fort McHenry NHS
and Historic Shrine

Winchester
Apple Blossom Festival
18th & 19th century buildings

Monocacy
NB

Inner Harbor
Art museums
Johns Hopkins University
Sports teams
Port

DELAWARE

ORCHARDS

Chesapeake and
Ohio Canal NHP

Rockville

Dover
State
capital

Cape May
Resort area
Victorian b

Front Royal

WASHINGTON

DC

Annapolis
State capital
U.S. Naval Academy
18th century buildings
Sailing & boating center

Cape
Henlope

Manassas
NB

St. Michaels
Maritime museum

Cape May-
Lewes Ferry

Alexandria
18th & 19th century buildings

Oxford
Ferry

DELAWARE

Shenandoah NP

HORSE
COUNTRY

Skyline Drive

Prince William
Forest Park

Thomas
Stone NHS

EASTERN SHORE

Ocean Ci
Resort area

PIEDMONT

TOBACCO
AUCTIONS

Salisbury
Poultry products

Assateague SP

Fredericksburg
Fredericksburg NMP
18th & 19th century buildings

St. Mary's City
17th century
colonial capital

Assateague
Island NS

Montpelier

George Washington
Birthplace NM

Stratford
Hall

Charlottesville
University of Virginia
Monticello & Ash Lawn

SEAFOOD
PRODUCTS

Chinco
NWR

VIRGINIA

TIDEWATER

Richmond
State capital
Richmond NBP
Maggie L. Walker NHS
Confederate capital
Museums

BAY

JAMES RIVER
PLANTATIONS

Williamsburg
Colonial Williamsburg —
restored 18th century capital
College of
William and Mary

To Appomattox
Court House NHP

Hopewell
Chemical
products

Yorktown
British surrender 1781
Colonial NHP

Cape Charles

ATLANTIC OCEAN

Petersburg
Petersburg NB
18th century houses

Jamestown NHS
17th century
colonial capital

SHIPBUILDING

Cape Henry

COUNTRY HAMS

HAMPTON
ROADS

Cape Henry Memorial

NORFOLK
Naval & maritime center
Adam Thoroogood House
Port

PEANUTS

North

0   10   50 Kilometers

0   10   50 Miles

Virginia Beach
Resort area

DISMAL SWAMP

NORTH CAROLINA

Beyond Washington the Middle Atlantic States are rich in history and natural beauty. It was here that the permanent settlement of America by Europeans began. The nature of the colonies' relationship to the Mother Country and to one another was debated in the various colonial capitals and in the homes of their leading citizens. Here the philosophical underpinnings of the new nation were hammered out and a war for independence was successfully prosecuted.

In a few days of sightseeing at National Park System sites and other areas, you can go from Jamestown, where English colonists first settled permanently; to Yorktown where the surrender of a British army made independence a reality; and to Philadelphia where the colonists severed their political ties with Great Britain, and where, several years after Yorktown, the delegates from the free and independent states hammered out the words of the Constitution.

In Baltimore you can see the fort where the bombardment took place that led to the writing of the "Star-Spangled Banner." Finally you can see some of the great Civil War battlefields where the nature of the Federal Union was tested by combat.

Besides all this historical heritage, the Middle Atlantic States offer an area of outstanding natural beauty, too. From the sandy shores of the Atlantic beaches to the ridgetops of the Appalachians you can find an appealing array of Eastern hardwood forests interspersed with long stretches of rolling farmland. Today these forests harbor a white-tailed deer population probably greater than when the first Europeans arrived.

More than 300 years of domestic architecture adds a distinctive touch to the landscape throughout the Piedmont of Virginia, Maryland, and Pennsylvania, and in fertile lands of the Shenandoah Valley of Virginia and West Virginia. The stone houses of southeastern Pennsylvania give way to the grand frame and brick dwellings of the Tidewater, which are in turn replaced by the solid brick and log farmhouses of the western valleys.

Chesapeake Bay exerts its pull on much of this land, too, for it is one of the world's great estuaries, with a shoreline several thousand miles long. The thousands of acres of wetlands renewed by the rise and fall of the tides are prime breeding grounds of the crabs and oysters for which the bay is justly famous. These same marshes, the hundreds of creeks and rivers draining into the bay, and a mild climate make this a major wintering ground for waterfowl. In the fall the air is filled with the sound of arriving ducks and geese as they glean the farm fields and settle down for the winter.

We usually think of cities as the home of distinct ethnic groups, but this region can lay claim to one of the few *rural* ethnic groups that exists in the United States: the Pennsylvania Dutch. They are German and not Dutch, that misunderstanding coming from English-speaking settlers' corruption of "deutsch," meaning German. For more than 200 years now, these people have maintained their language, religion, and way of life in a world that is increasingly at odds with their ideas. Their communities are centered on Lancaster County, Pennsylvania, a good day's outing from Washington.

Throughout these states the National Park Service cares for a number of natural and historical areas. Most of these parks are managed by the National Capital Region of the National Park Service. Besides all the parks listed in the gazetteer section of this book, there are three outlying parks worthy of your attention. Antietam National Battlefield, Maryland, and Harpers Ferry National Historical Park, West Virginia, commemorate events related to the Civil War and, at the latter, industrial history. See descriptions of them on pages 161 and 166. Catoctin Mountain Park is a forested haven for relaxation and recreation in northern Maryland. See the information on page 161. If you have the time, take a side trip to one or more of the areas described in the following pages. And if you do not have the extra time now, plan on visiting some of these places during your next trip to Washington.

A Note About This Map. Do not rely on this map to drive around the region. It is an introduction showing the locations of national parks and other sites along with some general notes about different areas. Study it before you set out and use it in conjunction with a detailed road map.

— **Robert Grogg, NPS writer-editor**

The pleasures of the country just north and east of Washington are the pleasures of wide open spaces and historic places, small town days and big city nights.

One relaxing spot is Assateague Island, an Atlantic barrier isle of beaches, dunes, and salt marshes where you can settle comfortably into a pace as easy-going as the flow of the tides. Seasonal flocks of snow geese, mallards, and other waterfowl grace the island's two major preserves—Assateague Island National Seashore and Chincoteague National Wildlife Refuge. Camp, fish, hike, bike, or canoe at the Seashore; at Chincoteague, don't miss the wild ponies made famous by the children's book *Misty of Chincoteague.* The manmade playground-resort of Ocean City—paradise lost to some, sun-and-fun capital to others—lies just to the north.

Further inland are the quaint villages and bustling metropolises surrounding Chesapeake Bay. Capt. John Smith declared the Chesapeake country a "delightsome land" in 1608, and it remains so today. The Eastern Shore, with its harbor towns of Oxford and St. Michaels, its scattered farms and wild lands, puts you in the down-to-earth company of fishermen, boatbuilders, and farmers. Across the bay is Annapolis, a thriving city since colonial days. Wander its historic streets, take in an outdoor art festival or boat show, or journey through three centuries of history-at-sea on a tour of the U.S. Naval

Above: Chincoteague ponies
Background: Chesapeake Bay

Academy. In Baltimore, visit the city's symbol of rebirth, Inner Harbor; shop, eat to your stomach's content, and go sightseeing at the National Aquarium and nearby Fort McHenry.

Many D.C. residents—even the President—like to escape to the Appalachian Mountains of Maryland for some R&R. While the President stays at well-guarded Camp David, ordinary folks can camp, hike, and, in winter, crosscountry ski next door in Catoctin Mountain Park. Two historic battlefields in the area—Antietam in Maryland, and Gettysburg in Pennsylvania—recall the sacrifices of two of the Civil War's bloodiest battles.

At Harpers Ferry National Historical Park in West Virginia, history and natural beauty converge. As you follow brick and cobblestone walks through this restored 1800s town, the Blue Ridge Mountains surround you. Frequent talks by park rangers shed light on the town's turbulent past: a 19th-century center for gun-manufacturing and storage, the site of abolitionist John Brown's raid in 1859, a strategic prize of Union and Confederate troops in the Civil War. Two mighty rivers, the Shenandoah and Potomac, meet here. Trails lead to outstanding views, and outfitters run raft and canoe trips. If you prefer hiking, the Appalachian Trail and the Chesapeake and Ohio Canal National Historical Park are just a footstep away.

— Carolyn de Raismes, **NPS writer-editor**

Virginia

The memorial to eminent Virginian Thomas Jefferson stands near one of the bridges linking Washington and Virginia. Jefferson, who had a strong hand in the planning of Washington and was the first President inaugurated here, embodies the deep-rooted ties between Virginia and the Nation's Capital. You can gain a deeper understanding of the city's sites by exploring Virginia's past.

Start with a trip through the Tidewater region. George Washington Birthplace National Monument (right) overlooks the Potomac below Fredericksburg, and a short distance downriver is Stratford Hall, where Confederate Gen. Robert E. Lee was born, as were his uncles Richard Henry and Francis Lightfoot Lee, signers of the Declaration of Independence.

Above: Oxen at George Washington's birthplace
Background: Gun crew at Colonial Williamsburg

Further south, just across the York River, lies Yorktown Battlefield, where General Washington accepted the surrender of British forces in 1781. This Revolutionary War site is connected by Colonial Parkway to Jamestown, where the story began 174 years earlier with the planting of the first successful English colony in America. Between them is Williamsburg (below), the restored colonial capital whose formal mall is echoed in L'Enfant's plan for Washington. Nearby Carter's Grove has been called the most beautiful of the Tidewater plantation houses.

Richmond's historic sites are worth the two-hour trip from Washington. At St. John's Church, Patrick Henry delivered his impassioned "Give me liberty or give me death" speech. Besides the National Battlefield Park, Civil War buffs will want to visit the White House of the Confederacy. Emblematic of the progress made by some blacks after the war is Maggie Walker National Historic Site, home of an ex-slave's daughter who became president of a bank. Richmond also has a rich architectural heritage. Jefferson himself designed the Virginia State Capitol.

Another enjoyable day trip takes you south along Skyline Drive through Shenandoah National Park for its views of the Shenandoah Valley. Turn east at Waynesboro and go to Charlottesville to visit the University of Virginia, another product of Jefferson's fertile mind, and Monticello, his hilltop home.

— *William Gordon*, **NPS writer-editor**

Philadelphia and Independence

A straight shot north on Interstate 95 from Washington takes the traveler to Philadelphia and Independence National Historical Park—the most historic square mile in the country.

Independence Hall (formerly the Pennsylvania State House) shines as the crown jewel of the park's cluster of historic buildings. It was in the Assembly Room, now restored, of this impressive Georgian building that the leaders of the Revolution adopted three of the Nation's most formative political documents: the Declaration of Independence, the Articles of Confederation, and the Federal Constitution.

Philadelphia served as the Nation's Capital for a decade, 1790-1800, while a new one was being built in the District of Columbia. Two buildings flanking Independence Hall were swept into federal service at this time. Congress Hall on the west became the meeting place of the House and the Senate, and the Old City Hall on the east became the seat of the Supreme Court.

Independence Square, the park-like setting for these venerable buildings, is itself two centuries old. In 1736 the Pennsylvania legislature declared the ground "a public open green" forever. By 1787, the year of the Constitution, a new landscaping plan graced the yard. Serpentine gravel paths leading through a variety of shrubs and trees made the square a restful place to stroll.

Everyone wants to see and touch the Liberty Bell, which is displayed in a pavilion north of Independence Hall. Cast in 1753 for the Commonwealth of Pennsylvania, the State House bell tolled on all public occasions— notably on July 4, 1776, at the first public reading of the

From left: Independence Hall, Liberty Bell, Assembly Room

Declaration of Independence. When a long-standing crack finally spoiled the tone early in the next century, the bell was retired from use. But abolitionists soon drew national attention to the bell when they claimed it as their symbol, citing its Biblical inscription, "Proclaim Liberty throughout all the Land unto all the inhabitants thereof." Thus Americans call it the Liberty Bell and hold it as an enduring symbol of American freedom.

Nearby Carpenters' Hall reminds us of the beginnings of the constitutional struggle with Great Britain. In 1774 the First Continental Congress gathered here to give voice to the colonists' mounting grievances against the mother country. The steps the delegates took led directly to the Second Continental Congress, which declared independence and launched the new nation.

Franklin Court delights visitors with a celebration of that many-sided genius, Benjamin Franklin. A steel frame in the interior court outlines his Philadelphia home, now gone. An underground museum portrays his career as a printer, scientist, politician, and diplomat.

Visitors to the park also can learn something of day-to-day living in 18th-century America. The Bishop White House, the home of the first Episcopal bishop in America, reflects the lifestyle of the affluent. The Todd House down the street was the home of John and Dolley (later Madison) Todd. You can catch a glimpse here of how a middle-income Quaker family lived.

— *Coxey Toogood*, **NPS historian**

165

Civil War Sites

Interested in the Civil War? Washington offers many attractions to satisfy your craving, among them Ford's Theatre, The House Where Lincoln Died, the Lincoln Memorial, and, across the Potomac, Arlington House, the onetime home of Robert E. Lee.

Beyond these, if you have the time, you might want to visit one or two of the battlefields maintained by the National Park Service within a few hours' drive of the city. Most feature self-guiding auto tours.

Perhaps the war's best-known battlefield is preserved at Gettysburg National Military Park, north of Washington in Pennsylvania. The battles fought here in July 1863 ended Robert E. Lee's second—and final—invasion of the North and marked the beginning of the end for the Southern Confederacy. The park also contains the national cemetery that President Abraham Lincoln

helped to dedicate on November 19, 1863, with his brief but enduring Gettysburg Address.

Antietam National Battlefield, northwest of Washington in Maryland, is almost as well known as Gettysburg. Here, on September 17, 1862, Lee's first northern invasion was turned back in the bloodiest single day's fighting of the war. Be sure to see the film at the visitor center.

Near Antietam, in West Virginia, is Harpers Ferry National Historical Park, scene of abolitionist John Brown's 1859 raid, which added to the atmosphere of hostility and fear that helped bring about the Civil War. Though not a battlefield in the traditional sense, the town was much fought over by both armies and changed hands many times.

In Virginia, southwest of Washington, Manassas National Battlefield Park commemorates two battles fought in the

Union and Confederate Civil War regalia and artifacts from national park collections

vicinity of a small stream known as Bull Run. The first, in July 1861, was the war's first major land battle; the second, on nearly the same ground just over a year later, cleared the way for Lee's first invasion of the North. Both were Union defeats.

The famous battlefields of Fredericksburg, Chancellorsville, the Wilderness, and Spotsylvania Court House are preserved south of Washington at Fredericksburg and Spotsylvania County Battlefields Memorial National Military Park. Several sites associated with Gen. George B. McClellan's 1862 Peninsula Campaign and Gen. Ulysses S. Grant's 1864 operations against Richmond and Petersburg can be found within Richmond National Battlefield Park south of Fredericksburg. The park's 57-mile auto tour route passes forts, trenches, and portions of the battlefields of Ellerson's Mill, Gaines' Mill, Cold Harbor, Seven Pines, Savage Station, Frayser's Farm, Malvern Hill, and others.

South of Richmond, Petersburg National Battlefield commemorates the 1864-1865 siege of Petersburg, where the last major Confederate stand of the Civil War took place. Don't miss the "War Room" and its audiovisual re-creation of the siege and events that led to the Confederate retreat from Petersburg and Lee's surrender to Grant at Appomattox Court House on April 9, 1865.

Appomattox is a little far for a side trip from Washington, but dedicated Civil War students will make the trip.

—*Raymond Baker*, NPS writer-editor

Washington provides countless vistas rich in beauty and historical connotations. From Arlington House—with its ties to the Washington, Custis, and Lee families and to the Civil War—the setting embraces the Kennedy graves in Arlington Cemetery, Memorial Bridge, the Potomac River, Lincoln Memorial, and numerous other sites commemorating major events and personages in our national heritage.

Index

Numbers in italics refer to photographs, illustrations, or maps. Generally, visiting hours and other information are listed on the same page as photos of a site.

Index

Index

Credits

Photographs and artwork not otherwise credited are from the files of the National Park Service.

Cover Robert Lautman; 2-3 Steve Gottlieb.

Part 1

4-5 Andrew Lautman; 6 Carol Highsmith; 8 Robert Lautman; 10 Robert Lautman; 12-13 © Robert Llewellyn; 15 Robert Lautman; 16 Robert Lautman; 18 Andrew Lautman; 20-21 Andrew Lautman; 22 © Robert Llewellyn; 24-25 Carol Highsmith; 26-27 Andrew Lautman; 29 Robert Lautman; 30 Robert Lautman; 32-33 Robert Lautman; 35 Chip Clark.

Part 2

36-37 Robert Lautman; 38-39 Robert Lautman; 40-41 Andrew Lautman; 42-43 Uniphoto; 44-45 Carol Highsmith; 46-47 R. R. Donnelley & Sons, Co.; 48 Mae Scanlan; 49-Statue of Freedom Robert Lautman; 50-51-L'Enfant Plan Library of Congress; 50-Diamond design Maryland Historical Society; 51-Thornton design Library of Congress; 52-53 Department of State; 54-55 U.S. Capitol Historical Society; 55-detail Mae Scanlan; 56-57 Robert Lautman; 58-59 Robert Shafer; 58-59-portraits National Portrait Gallery, Smithsonian Institution; 60-Folger Michael Freeman; 60-fountain Harry Abrams, Inc.; 60-Alice Paul Library of Congress; 61 Library of Congress/Stephen Shore; 62-63 Harry Abrams, Inc.; 64-Botanic Gardens Mae Scanlan; 64-Capital Children's Museum exterior Chip Clark; 65 National Portrait Gallery Smithsonian Institution/Robert Lautman; 67-Ford's exterior Andrew Lautman; 68-69 Robert Lautman; 69-Smithson National Portrait Gallery, Smithsonian Institution; 70-71 Smithsonian Institution; 71-sculpture Hirshhorn Museum and Sculpture Garden, Smithsonian Institution; 72-73 Air and Space Museum, Smithsonian Institution; 74-diamond Natural History Museum, Smithsonian Institution; 74-rotunda Chip Clark; 75 Museum of American History, Smithsonian Institution; 76 National Gallery of Art; 77 National Gallery of Art; 78-79 National Gallery of Art; 80-81 R. R. Donnelley & Sons, Co.; 82-83 United States Marine Band; 83-Blue Room National Geographic Society; 84-85 St. John's Episcopal Church; 85-inset burning of Washington Library of Congress; 86-87 White House; 87-*Resolute* Department of the Navy; 88 Mae Scanlan; 89-National Geographic Society Robert Lautman; 90-Renwick Robert Lautman; 90-91-desk Mae Scanlan; 91-museum Corcoran Gallery of Art; 92-desk Department of State; 95 Paula Wolfson; 96-97 Robert Lautman; 98-99 Mae Scanlan; 100-101 Robert Lautman; 102-103 Robert Lautman; 103-inset Museum of Fine Arts, Boston; 104 Greenhorne & O'Mara, Inc.; 106-107-Dumbarton Uniphoto; 110-street Uniphoto; 111-Islamic Center Mae Scanlan; 111-Shrine Mae Scanlan; 112 National Zoo, Smithsonian Institution; 113 Mae Scanlan; 114-museum Phillips Collection/Andrew Lautman; 116-117-Arboretum Lelia Hendren; 116-Cathedral Chip Clark; 117-Wilson House National Trust for Historic Preservation; 118-Barton house Robert Shafer; 118-119 Robert Lautman; 120-121 Robert Lautman; 122-trolley Mae Scanlan; 124-125-Arlington House Maxwell MacKenzie; 125-Arlington Cemetery Robert Shafer; 126-Carlyle House Mae Scanlan; 127-Masonic Memorial Mae Scanlan; 130-131 Robert Lautman; 133-Iwo Jima Memorial Marvin Wurtz.

Part 3

136-137 Andrew Lautman; 139 Robert Shafer; 141-band Andrew Lautman; 142-inset Smithsonian Institution; 144-Bartholdi fountain Robert Lautman; 146-147-Grant Memorial Robert Lautman; 148-149-actors Folger Theater; 149-dancers Paula Wolfson; 151-interior National Building Museum; 152-Capital Children's Museum Chip Clark; 152-clown Paula Wolfson; 153-children D.C. Committee to Promote Washington/Jim Marks; 154-155-embassy Robert Lautman; 156-157 D.C. Committee to Promote Washington; 158 Greenhorne & O'Mara, Inc.; 160-161-Chesapeake Bay Pamela Zilly; 162-163-gun crew © Robert Llewellyn; 164-aerial Robert Lautman; 164-165-Liberty Bell George Fistrovich; 165-Assembly Room George Fistrovich; 168-169 Staples & Charles.

★GPO: 1988 — 201-939-80001

National Park Service

The National Park Service expresses its appreciation to the many persons who made the preparation and production of this handbook possible. Countless organizations provided us with information and photographs to be used in the handbook, and we thank them all. The Service extends a special thanks to the Parks & History Association, a nonprofit organization that assists the parks in the National Capital Region with their interpretive efforts, for its financial support in obtaining texts, photography, and especially the work of Robert and Andrew Lautman, principal photographers for this book.

Library of Congress Cataloging in Publication Data
Washington DC: a traveler's guide to the District of Columbia and nearby attractions.
(Handbook; 102)
Supt. of Docs. no.: I 29.9/5:102
1. Washington (D.C.)—Description—Guidebooks.
2. Washington Region—Description and travel—Guidebooks. I. United States. National Park Service. Division of Publications. II. Series: Handbook (United States. National Park Service. Division of Publications); 102.
F192.3.W328   1988   917.53'044   87-600287
ISBN 0-912627-36-0